THE CHURCH THAT MIRACLES BUILT

Bob Hampton

For we walk by FAITH, not by sight.

2 Corinthians **5:7**

AbuzzPress

Published by Abuzz Press., St. Petersburg, Florida.

Printed on acid-free paper.

Abuzz Press / AbuzzPress.com
2018

First Edition

Dedications

In writing this book, I soon realized it was an ongoing work in progress. At some point, I needed to put down the pen and submit it. In a similar way, this book mirrors our lives, we are works in progress; I am a work in progress.

Therefore, I dedicate this book to the six churches I served as pastor; for they accepted me for who I was, yet encouraged me to become the man God designed me to be:

Calvary Bible Church, Whitehouse Station, NJ
Grace Bible Fellowship, Hillsborough, NJ
Mt. Eaton Church, Saylorsburg, PA
Lighthouse Reformed Church, Howard, PA
Carpenter's Community Church, Nazareth, PA
Faith Family Fellowship, Nazareth, PA

Acknowledgements

I begin with a sincere word of thanks to Abuzz Press in general, and Angela Hoy in particular, for providing the platform for this story to be told.

I remain indebted to four organizations and several people, too many to name here (but God and I know who you are) who were instrumental in making Faith Family Fellowship and its permanent home a reality.

First, I wish to thank Maranatha Family Christian Fellowship and Alexandria Manor for giving us a "home" until we had our own; and Beck's Land & Sea House and Jennings Transportation Corp. for giving us suitable parking for our congregants.

Further, I wish to thank three "English-proficient" friends who performed the first layer of editing:

Deb Piker, who surfaces in the story you are about to read; Linda Linton, a high school friend with whom I have reconnected after four decades and herself a published author; and

Christy Ayala, who worked through several layers of edits with me
and ultimately linked me with this publisher.
I also thank Glenn Restivo for pursuing his vision to start the church
around which this story is told.
Words fail me to express my heartfelt thanks
to my lawyer-friend of 33 years, Rich Hopkins,
who guided our church through the maze of legal documents.
I thank the entire church family at Faith Family Fellowship
for providing me the fodder for this story
and then encouraging me to write this book.
I thank both the Cover-Designer, Todd Engel, for his creative skills
and my Photographer son, Andrew Hampton,
who contributed the three cover photos.
Finally, and second only to God, I thank my wife of 12 years, Mari,
who supports me, inspires me, and serves alongside of me
in the greatest profession on earth.

Table of Contents

Prologue

I've never been caught up into Heaven by either an angelic escort or by a night dream. I've never witnessed a totally blind man gain instantaneous sight or an amputee sprout a replacement limb. I've never even heard of a casket lid ever flipping open and its former resident jumping out to conduct his own funeral. I've never experienced anything that defies the natural laws of science that can only be attributed to the powers of a supernatural Being. This said, I do believe in miracles of all kinds, but particularly of the more unremarkable variety that quietly slip in on us and too often pass undetected. I submit that if we're not primed with our heart's eyes, we will miss these Divine Love taps that remind us that God is alive, well and passionately interested in the affairs of a rather ordinary person like me - like you.

The true story I am about to share unveils two particularly remarkable miracles. But due to their stunning nature and precise timing, I suspect even skeptics may read away and scratch their heads bewildered. Oh, how I'd love for this tale to be the first step in a journey that lands the skeptic reader in a lifelong pursuit of the One he or she formerly doubted. But my equal hope, longs for the already-convinced to be encouraged in their faith-journey and propelled to look at life's circumstances with a more discerning eye. Why? Because in the invisible dimension cloaked behind the ordinary, God ceaselessly taps our spiritual shoulders with His Love. And every so often, He pulls off the dramatic that leaves our mouths agape and our hearts adoring.

To fully appreciate this story, however, it must be viewed against the backdrop of how for the past fifteen years, my life had been veering slowly, but steadily, off the track of what I was persuaded God had wanted me to do. Oh, not that I had caused this detour by stringing together a steady stream of poor choices, but rather like many of us, I had made one poor decision here and another there. Before long, however, my life was unraveling at every seam. The year was 2002 when the demolition crew of adversities began ripping down the edifice of my life. Little did I know at that time that the Master Architect was beginning to reconstruct, not just a whole new life for me, but even a brand-new church from His tool bag of miracles.

Chapter 1
Gifted at Failure

The EMTs untangled my unscarred legs from the steering wheel before sliding me onto the gurney and into the ambulance. The driver then slammed his foot onto the gas pedal and burned rubber for the next 5 miles across Route 80E. The race to the hospital seemed especially short for me as I teetered on the edge of consciousness. We had barely arrived at our cruising speed when the attendant who was stabbing me with several saber-sized needles yelled out, *"Let's boogie; we're losing him."* *("Did he think I was already unconscious??")* Now to most persons in my predicament, this announcement would've probably been met with probable fear and a sure-heightened sense of trepidation. But for me, *"H-e-a-v-e-n spelled relief"*.

Guess an explanation is in order. I hadn't been involved in a car crash; nor had I been abducted with my captors tying me in some contorted knot to the steering wheel. The pretzel effect made by the amalgamation of the steering wheel with my lower limbs was a design of my own imagination. *("Have I lost you yet?")* Maybe I need to rewind the tape and fill in the narrative gaps.

For months, I had been wallowing in the throes of a feeling-sorry-for-myself depression. My life had been coming unglued at every seam at an ever-accelerating pace - again. I didn't know if I could survive even one more emotional upheaval. So, no sooner had I pulled onto the entrance ramp of Interstate 80 for my daily commute to work, when my heart played its gymnastics tricks on me - again. Doing handsprings and backflips across the interior wall of my chest, while beating to the melody of an ever-slowing funeral dirge, I began to get light-headed - again. Though my car kept a straight path, the road before me spun around as though it had morphed into a circus merry-go-round. Not a comfortable feeling at 55mph. I deemed it wise to pull off onto the shoulder to spare other autos an unwelcomed meeting of the metals.

This occurrence had now become commonplace in my life over the past several months. And *"No"*, I had neither a drinking nor drug problem. But given my recurrent symptoms, you would have presumed I had visited my doctor, *"Right?"* No, not yet. *"Why not?"* Because she might just have diagnosed my ailment and provided me the cure. You're baffled and wondering, *"What is your problem?"* When you're seriously depressed and you see what might be the last light at the end of your life-tunnel, you welcome it - gladly, with open arms and tangled legs.

In the ensuing chapters, we'll retrace what led to such dejection, but for now, it's sufficient to say I was ready to go. Correction - I was eager to go. So, I turned off the engine, placed the keys where they were inconspicuous, but could be found by whomever would retrieve my car. Then I sat back and waited for the angels to carry me off to where depression never gains entrance.

But this is where my story degenerates into an enigmatic dilemma. Now I can't say how the depressed atheist may have handled this circumstance. But I suspect he would've smiled with the satisfaction that within moments, he would've ceased to exist and "entered" the "abyss" of extinction. Nor can I say how the depressed skeptic may have faced this trial. Perhaps he may have exacerbated his heart palpitations and sped up the inevitable because of his fear of the unknown and imminent future. Quaking, he would've exited into the who-knows-where? I, on the other hand, am profoundly religious. And yes, I know the world houses over 20 major religions and a plethora of many minor ones dotting the globe. So, let me make it clear that I do not see my ultimate existence as being absorbed into and made "one" with the universe. I do not see my "end" being repeated over and over again in the reincarnation cycle of a "Holy Cow" existence. Nor do I see my eternity ensconced by 36 pure virgins on either side of me. I believe in the Personal God reported in the Bible Who not only created us in His Own Image, but as revealed, has a specific and satisfying Plan for every person. Therefore, we should make it our life quest to invest all our spiritual energy into discovering exactly what that Plan is and doing all we can to make it happen.

So here was my profound conundrum: I believed God had sculpted me, complete with a blueprint for a specific purpose. Therefore, I should have been enthralled to enjoy such a privileged role in my infinitesimal corner within His Boundless Universe. But I was depressed - depressed to the point of wishing for death to snatch me away from my internal misery. Count on it: suicidal ideations plagued my daily routine on numerous occasions, blackening many a sunny day. But nope, I couldn't go there; I couldn't take my own life. Not that I was too scared to do so, but as disappointed as I was with myself, I was even less inclined to disappoint My Divine Designer. If I was one of His works of art on the highest rung of His Creation ladder, then how can I mar His masterpiece without thrusting my fist in His immaterial Face and in effect saying, *"You messed up!"*?

So, there I sat in my brand-new Chevy Tracker, lamenting over what I was certain was God's ongoing disappointment with me. I couldn't begin to count the number of times I had pled to Him to cart me off to His House of Bliss. The Bible teased me often with its consoling invitation to escape into Glory: *"He will wipe every tear from [my] eyes, and there will be no more death or sorrow or crying or pain. All these things are gone forever" (Revelation 21:4, NLT).* I loved the sound to that.

Now whether it was God's Holy Spirit prompting me or my own confounded and conflicted flesh baiting me, I don't know. But one of them convinced me to "barter" with the Almighty. (Probably not the Holy Spirit.) So, I offered a prayer that went something like this:

"Father, You already know what I'm thinking and how I've pled for over two years that You would take me Home. But if You're not finished with me yet - which I can't imagine as I feel I'm the personification of Failure - then You have 5 minutes before I call for an ambulance."
Nothing like pushing God into a corner under my terms and telling Him what the plan was going to be. Anyhow, this prayer set the stage for my pretzel-appearance. I was slowly ebbing away into the oblivion of unconsciousness, so I needed to ensure that I would still possess enough coherence to place the emergency call if God chose to preserve my life. I possessed enough mental acuity to know to place my legs over my head and let gravity do its thing. So, I hung my head over the passenger-side seat and "knotted" my legs in and through the steering wheel. I kid you not, I didn't cheat on even one second from this bargain. I remember fixating my eyes to my wristwatch. The first minute slowly ticked by, then a second and a third - with my cognitive clarity ever fading. By the fourth minute, my ability to focus was winding down faster than my watch. The fifth minute seemed to drag on interminably, but seared into my memory bank, I can still see those final ten seconds tick off vividly. Barely lucid by this point, I recall this *"Aha!"* moment when I felt more than a tad disappointed that Heaven would have to wait - at least for the next several minutes. Fortunately - or not - 911 on a touch screen is easy. Despite my slurred speech over my cell, the ambulance arrived in less than 5 more minutes and we were soon breaking the sound barrier as we raced in the direction of Pocono Medical.

I don't believe I ever lost consciousness as I vaguely recall being wired up to every cardiac piece of equipment and intravenous drip available in the ER. My blood pressure was falling off the gurney, only to be underperformed by my pulse. For the next few hours, my life teetered on the precipice of the afterlife. After my fluttering heart stabilized and my condition was upgraded from "Critical" to "Fair," the emergency team of doctors deemed it in my best interest to send me to another hospital that boasted one of the region's best cardiac-care units.

I guess this was comforting news, except for all the unanswered questions regarding my now uncertain future. Wouldn't you know, I'm going to live, but be incapacitated with a compromised heart for the rest of my life - and now, I'll probably live to be a centenarian. Great.

Between traffic accidents, sports injuries and a slew of sicknesses, the ER was spilling over with needing-to-tend-to bodies. When I was wheeled inside, there wasn't a single ER room available. The EMT's transferred me from their ambulance gurney onto the lone gurney in one of the hallways. Then I was stationed there until an attending physician could break free from his parade of patients. Meantime, a nurse saw that my gurney was in the way. It was impeding the flow of doctors and nurses scurrying between ER rooms. Not only so, all my equipment required an electrical outlet. So, she started to roll me - but to where? the only room available in the ER - a walk-in prostheses closet. She positioned me right in the center of the room, where all around me I was being stared down by artificial arms and legs, wall-to-wall replacement limbs. She then assured me a doctor would soon be in to see me as she shut the door behind her. I told her to shake a leg - she had every shape and size to choose from. She exited around 6:30pm.

At 7pm, the night shift came on duty; except for me. Somehow during the transfer of patient information, my name disappeared from the roster. At 1:30am, a nurse happened upon me, and with an incredulous, yet horrified look, she asked, *"What are you doing in here?"*

"Window shopping for a surrogate limb - if I ever need one." No, I didn't really voice that. But was she kidding? She didn't really think I wheeled myself in there, did she? Within a few moments, my room was flooded with staff and apologies. They even treated me to a mis-steak dinner.

Something else transpired during those seven "lost" hours that I never told them about. They were already embarrassed enough and fearing a lawsuit. Now this is not me, but they didn't know that. Picture yourself in my place, in that supine position - for seven hours - with IV cocktails flooding your veins. Yep. I had to pee - even before the day shift left! Now keep in mind, I was strapped down; I couldn't go (in both senses) anywhere. I know what you're thinking, *"Why didn't you yell for help?"* The simple answer is, I was drained of energy from the day's events, the door was shut, and I had no call bell. My shout might barely be recognizable as a loud whisper. By 9 o'clock, I'm squeezing my legs together and performing all sorts of other bladder-restraining maneuvers. 9:30 came and with it the contemplations of *"Why not just let go?"* Now I didn't want to be the one embarrassed - nor did I want to lay in my own Swine Lake.

At 9:30-something, I had made my decision; one that showcased my improvisational skills. I scanned the wall, shimmied my gurney toward my selected target and plucked out of obscurity the first-ever elbow-bedpan. With precious little time to spare, I had cradled it where it needed to be and soon I was thanking the Lord for that pause that spells relief.

Problem solved - well, not totally. Where do I empty my "relief"? There's not even a trash can in this room, much less any lavatory facilities. The irony of the moment seized me. I repressed the urge for hours and devised this ingenious plan, only to spill my "relief" all over me in the middle of the night. Process the obvious here. The only way I was going to prevent spillage was to cradle my elbow all night long while staying awake. But I was already beyond tired from my long and adventuresome day. I did well. Necessity proved once again the mother of invention; it also proved the father of perseverance. Now think me crazy, but at 1:30 when I was discovered, I hid my "relief" under my sheet. What was I thinking? Who knows by this time in my ordeal? I think it was more than just embarrassment; I believe it was for fear I might be charged with some rare-cited hospital misdemeanor for *wetty* larceny. What I do know is that I cradled my greased elbow till morning when a friend of mine arrived and I transferred the not-goods to her. She disposed of the evidence, scrubbed my "savior" and tucked it under my gurney. I'm sure some nurse eventually found it and wondered what it was doing on the floor. (I'm hoping she never reads this book.) No doubt she washed, sterilized and remounted it on my wall of shame. I've often wondered who might have benefitted from the extra elbow grease – uh, never mind.

I learned much later, in fact, 6 months later, when I made a repeat performance of this my debut hospitalization, that it was no cardiac infarction that almost did me in, but the "silent killer" of carbon monoxide poisoning. Hindsight betrayed the greater wisdom to lift weights with sufficient spatial separation between me and a kerosene heater in a well-ventilated space. Duh.

As lucidity returned, I deduced that God wasn't finished with me yet. I got that, but discovered in the aftermath that failures would continue to haunt my plans.

There's a movie I must have watched a dozen times or so and will see it a dozen more. Despite knowing the outcome before I ever watched the film, and the outcome has never flinched with any of my repeated viewings, *Apollo 13* still captivates me. Who will ever forget that non-negotiable decree during the height of the crisis from Flight Director, Gene Kranz? He said something we all wish would always be true in every area of our lives: *"Failure is not an option!"* Reality, however, proves to be far less gracious.

I remember the noted radio preacher, Chuck Swindoll, once offering these perplexing words that have resonated and stuck with me ever since. He said, *"Our problem isn't that we've failed; it's that we haven't failed enough."* What he meant is that failures provide this marvelous opportunity to learn life lessons more quickly and more profoundly than successes. Well then, given this formula, I must've been poised to have been very successful, the prize float in a parade of failures. I agree with Mr. Swindoll. I don't remember having received many good grades during my schooling. And yes, I did have some. But I sure do remember the "F" I received for my 8th grade book report on *"Gone with the Wind"* and the "37" I received on a 10th grade Social Studies test. Now a "37" would be an acceptable score if it had been out of a possible "50". No, I earned a "37" out of a possible "100". *"Is there such a grade as an F--?"* I don't remember the hits I contributed to our high school baseball team - and I should because they were so few and far between. But I do remember my last at bat my senior year, striking out with the bases loaded on a 3-2 slider. *(What high school pitcher throws a 3-2 slider with the bases loaded???)* I don't remember many of my first dates during those traumatic teen years, but I do remember my last date with each of those 11 girls who dumped me. I obviously learned a lot in life - because I failed so often. Some would argue I'm gifted at failure.

But these failures are inconsequential; these failures are of such minor import in the perspective of the whole of life. For the flight crew of Apollo 13, however, failure translated into disaster, whether from being hopelessly lost in space until the oxygen supply dissipated or to disintegrating upon reentry into the earth's atmosphere. Failure can be catastrophic. But it can also be instructive - and should be. In my life, it has been just that - a lot. So, though Gene Kranz's dictum applied during that *failed* trip to the moon, but *successful* ride home, failure isn't always a bad thing. Our success-driven culture has immunized us from accepting any kind of failure. I believe we have done our people a disservice because I am fully persuaded that *"failure is an option"*.

Chapter 2
Failure and Me - Imperfect Together

Striking out at the plate in a public forum or with the fairer sex in a private setting is no big deal (though at the time of both, I felt my world imploding!). But I also struck out in the two areas that perhaps most would agree are preeminent among all the rest. Now I know I'm not alone in either; and many greater and wiser people than me have fallen further and harder. But failure doesn't grade on a curve. It cares less if mine has weighed in at less of a failure than somebody else's. I failed, I know it and I bear the repercussions from it. So, this is my condensed story about failure at home and at work.

Failure at Home

Many concur with the familiar adage, *"Love is blind"* - until it's *them* we're talking about. They may confess to a mild philamyopia. (Yep, made that word up; but Webster would do well to incorporate it in his next edition.) It's when we enter a romantic relationship and can't see (choose not to see?) anything beyond the immediate. We're shortsighted and can't see (won't look?) down life's road.

Now it's not like I had raced down the marital aisle. Following high school, I had trekked off to college with more than just an educational objective in view. I knew I had the next four years, 20 tops, to date around with a discerning eye for that potential life partner - and I do mean *life* partner. I believed in the familiar *"till death do us part"* coda to virtually every marriage ceremony.

In my sophomore year I had met and started dating this young college coed who had caught my eye. We dated for four years; even taking a hiatus in the middle from the romance to test our hearts elsewhere by dating around. We thought it may be better to assess the quality and durability of our relationship from a distance. Now every relationship encounters bumps and potholes along the way, but we seemed to navigate over or around them. Besides, we were young and immature. Time and experience would mature us to rise to the lifetime commitment. So, proceeding to the next step along the romance continuum, I got down on my one knee and proposed - ready or not.

For the ensuing 28 years, it seemed that more bumps and potholes sprang up along our marital journey, with few ever being hurdled or sidestepped - much less resolved. I grew weary. But of course, my self-justifying ego constantly raced to its own defense, silently murmuring, *"It's mostly her fault;"* or at least the more sizeable chunk of blame falling on her side of the guilt-ledger. Funny how adept we all appear to be in identifying the flaws in our spouse, while wearing blinders to our own. But I ask myself, *"Does this really matter? Does it really make any difference to determine whether I was 43% or 93% guilty?"* It takes two to mess up a marriage. It's never the exclusive fault of but one. So regardless of the percentile differential, I shared part of the breakdown-responsibility. Now I can keep passing the buck of fault to assuage my own culpability, but I keep getting a pocketful of change in return.

I have no intention of building a case here to seek some level of justification for why I threw in the marital towel. The Bible explicitly declares, *"I hate divorce, says the Lord."* (Malachi 2:16). So, no degree of rationalizing, marginalizing, legitimizing, sanitizing or even vaporizing the biblical revelation on the subject can excuse my selfish choice. I knew the Divine perspective. Consequently, I knew I was disappointing my Creator and the Designer of marriage. Now I don't state this casually, much less flippantly; I struggled more over how I was hurting God than my wife.

Every marriage totes tattered "baggage" into the new union. This is simply because marriage brings together two imperfect people. I slung three "bags" of my own imperfections onto what would eventually ignite into a funeral pyre. The first dilapidated bag I brought along was my own unfiltered negativity. We're all familiar with the *"half full-half empty cup"* to indicate one's optimism versus pessimism. My cup is bone dry. I can be so negative, I'm absolutely positive I'm completely negative. Granted, some of this finds its origins in my staunch upbringing and my parents' bent towards religious legalism - which then bent me in that direction. But no, I'm not blaming them.

A sizeable share of my negativity can also be traced back to my DNA - it's who I am; it's how God wired me. No, I'm not blaming Him either - as I don't like the prospect of being struck by lightning (see, I told you I was negative). But in identifying both my parents and God's contributions to why I am who I am, I'm neither signaling them as my scapegoats nor am I excusing myself of culpability. I recognize my negative proclivity and know I must combat it as a matter of daily course.

So, when my then-wife did something I deemed inappropriate, I creatively put a negative spin on her behavior. Oh, this must have endeared her to me! *"You always ..."* or *"You never ..."* dotted the landscape of my interaction with her in the early years. By the later years, there was very little interaction of any kind.

Why are people like me so negative? I suspect several factors can account for this character flaw. I offer here just a sampling: First, coupling my theological persuasion of man's depravity with his constant confirmation thereof, reinforces my negativity. I'm convinced that because man is bad, he can't help but perform badly. The only good news in this is that nothing ever blows me away. Nobody can do anything so abominable that I'd be left speechless, dumbfounded by somebody's atrocity. But this is no real salve.

Another factor, much to my shame, revolves around my competitive bent. If I put others down, it's probably due to a subliminal grasp to push myself up. Stupid. Just plain stupid. Over time, the Bible has convicted me to start filling my empty cup by choosing to speak positively. A verse that continues to curb my dialogue reads: *"Let everything you say be good and helpful, so that your words will be an encouragement to those who hear them" (Ephesians 4:29).* Even the salient counsel from the sheepish rabbit (half-breed?) from Disney's *"Bambi"*, Thumper, keeps caroming off my mental cubicles, *"If you can't say somethin' nice, don't say nothin' at "all".*

Here's one more factor: When you fail, you inhale those negative fumes of distrust and deprecation. And when you fail repeatedly, you absorb them into the very fabric of your psychosocial being. I was not surprised to learn the first time I donated blood some 40 years ago, that my blood type is 0-Negative. It figured. But God has been performing His psycho-pulmonary work on my life and exchanging my negative fumes with His positive virtues. He has primarily accomplished this through a heightened revelation regarding His Grace. The Bible teaches that He views me through the blood-spattered lenses of His Son's finished work on an ancient cross. Accordingly, God sees all Jesus' merit credited to me. The negative sinful person that I am is seen by the Father as the positive sinless person that His Son is. So, for me to interpret life negatively spurns the great work Jesus did in filling my cup to overflowing. About this, I'm positive!

Another piece of tattered luggage I brought into the marriage was my perfectionism, that subliminal rigidity that doesn't accept anything that isn't done *"right"*. Of course, this raises one's eyebrows in concert with the question, *"Who determines what is right?"* I do! - and so does every other perfectionist. Hmm. How about if two perfectionists disagree on a subject? Who then is correct? Obviously, I am; for all the others aren't as perfect as this perfectionist. (Each would make the same case.)

Now once you clear this first objectionable hurdle and acquiesce to the perfectionist's myopia, a second one readily surfaces. If I read your mind aptly, it's wrestling over an apparent contradiction: *"Now wait a minute, you just got done spelling out your negativity, yet you demand perfection."* I hear you. But actually, the two subjects cohabit rather comfortably. When you demand perfection of yourself and fall short of your self-imposed and improbable standards, and you keep falling short, the mind naturally slips into a defeatist mentality. Like a lazy raincloud creeping overhead, a negative disposition slowly drifts towards and eventually hovers over one's mental outlook.

With no slight against my parents, they reared me in that 1950's stereotypical Baptist mindset that massaged my perfectionist bent. How'd they do this? By assisting God in clarifying the obvious intent of the Ten (Plus) Commandments. For example, the Fourth Commandment in our home read, *"Honor the Sabbath Day by wearing a white shirt, tie and jacket to church and keeping the TV off all that day into the morrow."* Our Seventh Commandment read, *"Thou shalt not smoke or chew or go with girls who do; for in the day that thou eatest thereof, thou shalt surely die."* My mom piggybacked on this frightful revelation with the reminder that it lay in her Divinely-ordained prerogative as the *"one who brought me into this world"*, she could also be God's instrument as the *"one who takes me out."* Yea, my legalistic upbringing fueled my perfectionism.

Now if I find any trace of consolation in owning up to my debilitating perfectionism, it's in knowing I demand it only of myself. I don't impose my ludicrous standards onto others, and I strove not to do so on my "ex". However, when living under the same roof, how could she not have felt the unspoken pressure of my silent example? So, as I painted a "perfect" line along the chair rail, or penned the "perfect" sympathy card or folded my underwear in the only "perfect" manner, my actions screamed a louder message than any words. Though I didn't command perfection from my wife, she likely assumed I had; and the marriage continued to erode.

The third piece of ragged luggage I carried to the altar was one that beguiled me without mercy. For something else woven into the fabric of who I am is this compassionate heart. *"That's a good thing, right?"* Not if you allow it to delude you into thinking better of yourself than you really are. I "saw" some Messiah-powers in me that could "fix" anything I concluded needing fixing in her. Oh, how naive and vain we can be! I discovered you don't commit to a marriage if you can't accept the intended exactly the way he or she is and/or believe too strongly in your own limited abilities. There is but one Messiah and I'm not He!

I can't blame anyone else for my negativity, perfectionism or Messiah-complex. These were my sins; my faults that only widened the ever-growing fissure in my marriage.

Given this schism, something all-too-common began to rear its ugly head in my life. As time passed after my wife and I had exchanged our wedding vows, and dissatisfaction displaced the idealism of newlyweds, my heart drifted onto the turf of the *"greener grass"*. Now before your curiosity so sidetracks you into going where it naturally wants to go, I'll answer your unasked question: *"Yes, I committed adultery. And no, I did not commit adultery."* *"What?"* Allow me to answer the question another way, *"It all depends on whose definition of adultery one is using."* By most everyone's definition, I did not commit adultery. I didn't even dally in foreplay, let alone go the distance. But I don't live by "most everyone's definition". I live by the one Jesus espoused. He was quoted by one of his closest companions when He had preached publicly on the subject: *"I say, anyone who even looks at a woman with lust has already committed adultery with her in his heart."* I plead *"Guilty"*. In fact, given Jesus' definition, I plead *"Guilty"* for countless violations.

I dared not surf the Internet or scan the magazine racks to pour any more visual fuel onto the glowing embers of my lust. I have seen too many lives and marriages train-wrecked by heading down that one-way track. I also established even "higher" and more "impenetrable" boundaries to keep me "safe". Chalk this up to my perfectionism. But nobody can avoid every billboard along the highway or every encounter, random or scheduled, with a fairer-sex coworker or church friend. Some degree of contact with the opposite sex is inevitable. So, knowing my own vulnerability and masculine inclinations, I went overboard in trying to do *"right"* - and in this case, *"right"* is universally accepted.

After 28 years, however, I ended the marriage. I chose divorce, something this strongly religious perfectionist never imagined he'd do. This guy who still believes God can do the impossible, shelved the Omnipotence of God for a time. I quit on the possible miracle-in-the-making. God could have fixed the marriage. Cognitively, I knew that even then. But emotionally, my inner pain was crying out so loudly, I had gone deaf. I couldn't see myself enduring another year, another month, another day. Long story short, in marriage I failed my spouse. In divorce, I failed my God.

Making the decision to divorce had become so much harder when Andy, our first and only child, entered the family portrait. Prior to getting married, we had dreamed of parenting four children. We even had their names picked out - which presupposes their sexes too: a pair of each. But after navigating our way through turbulent waters from Day 1, our desire for children - and each other - evaporated. But after 16 years into the marriage, Andrew came as a shock and nothing short of a shock! No irreverence intended here, but whereas Jesus entered the world via the immaculate conception, Andrew entered the world through an impossible conception. Or not.

Fast forward now seven years to the separation and two more to the divorce. You can imagine the degree of self-flagellation I imposed when I left home. I know what many of the studies indicate: that a bad marriage is better for children than a broken one. Confessedly, I teemed with a mishmash of doubts over that. Nevertheless, being the negativist,

I beat myself up as the absentee father; and this absentee father failed his perfectionist bent.

I plummeted even deeper into depression when I exited the marriage. I couldn't even "fix" myself, let alone my wife. I failed, and I failed but good - which is bad, real bad.

Failure at Work

When life spirals out of control at home, many retreat to their place of employment for reprieve. These persons find their much-needed affirmation, the strokes that keep them on a semi-even keel in life, in what they do Monday through Friday. But for me, the workplace only magnified my failure exponentially. And why? Because of my chosen field.

It may be true of other professions, but is certainly true of mine, that the employer gets *"two for the price of one"*. Despite the courting dialogue during the interview process and the pre-hire assurances to the contrary, from Day 1 on the job, my new employer, a church, didn't just get a new *pastor*, they got a husband and wife *team*. Granted, I don't remember reading even one requirement spelled out in any church Constitution for my spouse; but I do remember hearing the constant barrage of second and third-hand murmurs of displeasure – justified or not: *"Why isn't the pastor's wife going to ...?" "Shouldn't that be the job of the pastor's wife?" "She shouldn't say things like that, she is the pastor's wife."* Now tack on the biblical injunction that the pastor must *"manage his own family well ... for if he can't, how can he take care of God's church?"*, I was doomed to fail at work too. So, I'm saddled in a marriage I lamented that's being lived in the fishbowl of my workplace for all the church to see. Instead of being my safe haven, my workplace became the magnified mirror of my dismal failure at home.

Couple my growing dissatisfaction with an even greater proportion of guilt, my effectiveness took a nosedive. For example, how do you provide healthy, objective counsel to a starry-eyed pair looking to wed or to an embattled couple looking to unwed? How do you mount the pulpit proclaiming, *"Husbands, love your wives as Christ loves His Church"* (see Bible: Ephesians 5:25) and not feel the searing guilt of conspicuous hypocrisy? How do you lead your leaders to live *"above reproach"* when you loathe yourself for your life of self-contradiction? How do you model Jesus Who personified love, grace, patience and forgiveness before your entire congregation when your heart is spilling over with bitterness, condemnation, impatience and mercilessness towards your spouse?

I can honestly say I am profoundly grateful for every church I've pastored. They served me in the very virtues I had failed to serve them. They fleshed out the love, grace, patience and forgiveness towards me that I found so hard to exercise towards my wife. Yet they understood their greater responsibility to the whole church as opposed to this singular member of it. So, for the greater good of the entire worshiping community, this translated into, *"You have to go."* One church had put me on sabbatical with the intent to assist me in ironing out my home failures. Another church made the harder choice to drop the curtain on my ministry. Both churches had tried other therapeutic measures before pulling the hard string - because of love, grace, patience and the willingness to forgive. 20+ years later, I remember the exact words of one elder, Rod, lamenting the decision he knew he had to make in terminating my pastorate; but words that reflected his heart of Jesus-like compassion. He had said, *"If I vote with my heart, you stay. But if I vote with my head, you go. I hate voting with my head."* But I had been the failure, a repeat offender, not he. He was performing his biblical obligation.

A failure at home and at work, the two premier venues where we all most covet success. *"Maranatha - come quickly, Lord Jesus; and if not for Your Whole Church, at least for me!"*

Chapter 3
Failure and RCO's

Being the *"empty cup"* guy, I didn't naively presume that ending my marriage would end either my depression or my problems. The former only deepened while the latter multiplied. In a matter of just a few months, I had "lost" my family, my house, my job, and yes, even my career. In the ministry, divorce does not bode well on one's resume. My marketability mirrored the attraction of a pig roast at a Bar-mitzvah.

I also experienced the "fair weather" friends' syndrome. But in deference to the conundrum into which we had all plummeted, I found myself quite alone. It wasn't like most of them didn't like me anymore; though several expressed their disappointment. They just weren't sure how to act around me or what to say. As one of them timidly confessed to me, *"I feared that whatever I said to you would only make matters worse. There were many times I wanted to reach out; but how do you counsel your counselor? How do you pastor your pastor?"* Two couples risked the awkward circumstance and proved to be my "tempest weather" friends. They did reach out - and regularly. I spent many an afternoon or evening just vegetating in the comfort of Clyde and Charlene's or Gary and Sally's homes. How refreshing to be embraced when what I most needed wasn't more rejection, much less lecture, but a hug, an ear, and an extravagantly moist slice of triple chocolate cake - with lavishly thick milk chocolate icing.

Consequently, during the last week of 2000 as the world eagerly anticipated the new millennium (unlike the pervasive fear the year prior with Y2K), I lay curled up in the fetal position for seven days. I didn't eat, and I barely drank any fluids. When healthy, the needle on the scale pointed between 150 and 155 lbs. Now I weighed a cadaverous 130 lbs. - in full winter regalia. Was I subconsciously assisting God with expediting my premature demise? Probably. Of course, we're talking here about the week when Christians around the globe celebrate Jesus' birth and the world counts backwards from Ten to welcome in a new year with great expectations! Then to magnify my pain, in the center of that week, on the 28th, I "celebrated" my 46th birthday - devoid of family, friends, cake and presents. I sang silently to myself, *"Crappy birthday to me. Crappy birthday to me. I feel like a failure, and look like a zombie."*

The next day, I received a call from a friend who invited me to his house to attend a New Year's Day party. He and his wife - a very happily married couple I might add (*"Why would I torture myself by socializing with success?"*) - often invited upwards of 25 people to come over and enjoy each other's company and various holiday celebrations. John and Sandy were fully aware of my fragile state and suspected that if I continued to languish in that condition, they'd be attending my impending funeral. John knew I needed to get up, get moving and get help. Evidently, he had thought through this carefully; so, he capitalized on my love for football. Everybody knows Bowl Games dominate the TV schedule every New Year's Day. He called and dangled the football-carrot before me. I responded, *"John, I appreciate your invitation, but I'm really not up for it."* I had lost my sanity. This was certainly a first-for-me, to pass up a guy-gathering to watch football!

He countered with something like, *"Bob, you really need to get up and about. This'll be good for you."*

Not to be coerced from my resolve, I fired back, *"John, you know I'm a mess. I wouldn't want to ruin the fun for everybody else."*

He jarred me with his comeback: *"There's not going to be any party; we canceled it, so you're coming over."* How do you say, *"No"* to a couple who are so selfless and caring as this? It took every fiber of my determination to crawl out of bed, get dressed, fall into my car and drive the 3-mile route to John and Sandy's on the 1st. It also took the preceding 3 days to force-feed those every fibers.

Immediately it felt good to be accepted and loved. Not to my surprise, we watched very little football that day; but we did talk a lot. John and Sandy gave me the hug and the ear I so desperately needed. I didn't even miss the extravagantly moist slice of triple chocolate cake - with lavishly thick milk chocolate icing. Okay, maybe a little.

John didn't retreat from his primary objective: to ensure that I seek help and get prescribed an anti-depressant regimen. He was eager to drive me that day to the psych unit of our local hospital. But as one can expect, I was reticent. Many deflect their need to confront their problems, while some won't even admit to them. These two issues weren't mine. I had serious problems and I knew I had them. I just didn't want to face them any longer. But as a minster who for years had trumpeted the all-sufficiency of the Omnipotent God, my issue revolved around the seeming contradiction to what I preached and what had degenerated into my practice. I pled to John, *"I've preached throughout my career that Jesus is all we need for our every problem. And you know me, I'm not opposed to advising people to take prescribed psychotropic meds. But please grant me 30 days to trust God to start the healing process in me now that He has used you to grab my full and fixed attention. And if after 30 days, you don't observe a decided upswing in my mood, then you can transport me wherever you deem best."* John would've preferred making the trip to the psych ward that day as he feared in 30 days my trip would be to the morgue; but he acquiesced.

30 days later, not only John, but all who knew my circumstance perceived God was doing a work! He proved Himself once again as the Divine Healer.

My problems didn't evaporate. But my attitude sure did! complemented by an ever-soaring trust in the God-of-All-Mercy-and-

Grace. What I once preached in theory, I could now report from experience. Over the next few months, but certainly by summertime, I was enjoying life once again. No, not because I had returned to ministry, because churches don't flock to the hire of recent divorcees. My pastoral career was on hold - at least temporarily, if not permanently. My new career path in the mental health profession helped me to cope with the realization that I had failed in marriage. (Had I, in an ironic twist of destiny, become my own counselor?) Nonetheless, I accepted this new direction as God's Second-Chance Will for my life.

This discovery bordered on *revolutionary* for me. I knew God had granted Moses a second chance as he attempted several excuses. *"You've got the wrong guy, Lord. I'm no deliverer."* But when bushes speak, especially incombustible, flaming ones, people listen. (See Bible: Exodus 3) I knew God had granted Jonah a second chance after he had hightailed it in the opposite direction. But God hailed down a limo-fish to taxi Jonah to the shore-step of Nineveh. (see Bible: Jonah 1) I knew God had granted Peter a second chance after having denied any consorting with the *"Galilean."* A simple instruction to drop his net on the opposite side of his boat, yielding a net-tearing over-haul of filets, restored Peter's call to be a *"fisher of men."* (See Bible: John 21) But in each of these cases, God performed an unquestioned miracle. Not so with me. No flaming foliage. No cabby-carp. No gross *net* income. Nevertheless, His Merciful Heart reached down with His Healing Hand and granted me a second chance.

My career in professional ministry had come to a disheartening halt. But ministers do not possess the exclusive reserve on ministry. Ministry belongs to every believer in Jesus. So, I merely exchanged the venue of where I mounted my pastoral pulpit. I gathered my new "congregation" from among my mental health coworkers who strove to rescue hurting people from the morass of their poor choices. *("Talk about a right fit for me. Been there - done that. I could counsel from experience!")* Granted, they hardly shared any of my ideological persuasions, and whereas I lived by "The Good Book", they lived according to the *"Diagnostic and Statistical Manual of Mental Disorders, Volume 4"*. Yet despite our differing resource authority, we all shared the no-brainer recognition that people screw up. We may have begun from different launch points, but we all docked at the same therapeutic port. Whereas they attributed anomalistic behavior to good people going wrong, I attributed it to bad people acting naturally. Whereas they believed we can fix ourselves with the proper protocol of therapy and medication cocktails, I believed that ultimately it is God Who fixes what's broken within humanity. So, my "church" wasn't populated with persons who necessarily believed in the same things I do, but I still got to minister!

Sunday "Church" still meant the world to me. No, I wasn't leading a flock anymore, but I was enjoying my new role in the pew. Even through my year-long depression, I don't think I missed but one or two worship services. On those day when I felt most down, I forced myself to get up. I never regretted making that extra effort because I always came away refreshed in spirit. I was discovering that many of the principles I used to preach, proved to be better than I had proclaimed them.

I knew I needed to plug into a local church somewhere, not just because I understood its therapeutic value, but I also believe it pleases God when we pour our heartfelt energies into the one organization He founded. So, I began to visit several in the general vicinity. Were there certain features that would aid my search? Sure. I like contemporary Christian music. I enjoy small groups that meet during the week. I insist on expository Bible preaching, which is a fancy way of saying I want to hear the Bible taught literally, and in a manner, I can apply it to my life practically.

I could have joined every church I had visited, were it not for this one disturbing similarity. I'd inconspicuously slip in and find a seat. I'd bow my head and ask my Heavenly Dad to prepare my heart for worship. Almost without exception, someone would approach me, many folks I didn't even know, and say, *"Pastor Bob, how are you?"* Then they'd unveil just enough that let me know they knew more than I wish they knew about my recent history: divorced and defrocked. Then my mind reeled with all sorts of *"What have they heard?"* questions; which when a minister steps out of ministry typically means one of two things: either he ran off with the church's money or the church's secretary - or both. It didn't matter that I knew neither were true. It didn't even concern me what conclusions these folks had drawn; because people will believe what they want to believe, and I didn't have a sufficient reserve of emotional energy to launch my own defense; nor was that my responsibility. Vindication's in God's court. I often echoed the Psalmist's innermost cry: *"'Vindicate me. O God!' - 'cause if You don't, the rumor mill will only grind out more spicy fodder for hungry hearts to devour."* What mattered to me was that every week I was reduced to tears. I found it nearly impossible to worship without my past regurgitating before me. Just 3 months into my search, I realized I needed to commute beyond the general vicinity to find a church family who didn't know me (or the juicy rumors swirling about me) from Adam - except that I had far fewer wrinkles.

Someone had told me about a church she thought I might like; and it was a blessed 40-minute drive! Rather ironic in that I had always told people searching for a new church home to limit their search to a 5-mile radius. I believe in the *local* church - well until now. On February 4, 2001, I visited Carpenter's Community Church. It was larger than I would have preferred. But perhaps this too was providential. I could hide. Ofttimes the best place to hide is in a crowd. But before I proceeded with my Sunday routine of inconspicuously slipping into a seat, I scanned the sanctuary - thoroughly. *("Great! I don't recognize a soul!")* I sat down and started to pray. Then I felt a tap on my shoulder. Immediately my prayer changed to, *("That better be You, Lord!")* A female voice denied me any such hope. *"Hi Pastor Bob. How are you? I heard all about ..."* I was pretty good - up until that moment.

I managed to shake this initial upset and settle into worship. I particularly enjoyed the music! Now this isn't some gracious way to state that I didn't like the preaching; it was fine. It's just that the guy behind the pulpit that day wasn't the guy who usually occupied it. The church was featuring a guest missionary speaker. So, between wanting to hear the pastor preach and being enticed by the music, a second visit was warranted. But as I was exiting the building, the pastor of the church, though playing hooky from the pulpit but not from attendance, didn't let me slip out unwelcomed. No big deal, I'll play that PR game, then quietly shuffle to my car.

Offering his hand for a shake, he introduced himself, *"Hi, I'm Jim Grimes. You don't look familiar to me. Is this your first time with us?"*

"As a matter of fact, yes." Now because I had been on the opposite side of this handshake for most of my adult life, and desperately wanting to make a quick and anonymous exit, I added what I knew he most wanted to hear. *"I enjoyed the service; I'm just sorry that I didn't get to hear you preach, but I'll be back next week."* I would've left at that point, except he still had my hand; and he wasn't letting go. He fished for more. *"Just great,"* I mused.

"What's your name?"

"Bob."

Evidently, that wasn't good enough. Then there was this sustained moment of quiet. I attempted to leave. He still clutched my hand.

After a few more uncomfortable moments, he broke the silence, *"Do you have a last name?"*

He knew I did and I couldn't lie, so I answered his question, *"Yes."* Another sustained moment of discomforting quiet.

"May I ask what it is?"

"Really! You're not getting this - that I want out - now!" No, I didn't prove that rude by voicing this desperate dodge. I knew I had to fill in his blank with something, but with my heart rate escalating to near-stroke levels, I dittoed my former inane answer: *"Yes."* Perhaps I was thinking, *"Sure, you have the perfect freedom to inquire as to my last name; but I sure ain't telling you what it is - just in the event the rumor mill has tendrils that have descended all the way down from the Poconos into the Lehigh Valley."*

Man! was he obnoxiously relentless. *"Well?"*

With a whisper, I came clean. *"Hampton."* Evidently my whisper had been too soft because he asked me to repeat it. I came even cleaner. *"Hampton, Bob Hampton."*

There are moments in all our lives when we look for that hole within which to crawl. This was one of my myriad of those moments - especially of late. Oh, how I craved that this was the *hole-iest* church I ever visited. Not only did Jim's as-big-as-saucer eyes betray he knew something, but his words, forever seared into my conscience, confirmed he did. *"Oh, you're Bob Hampton! I heard ..."* You've got to be kidding me. I'm a near-nobody - except in God's eyes - with not a lot of natural talent, very average leadership skills and as run-of-the-mill preaching prowess as the next pastor. But light the match of a good juicy rumor and the sky is soon ablaze with the inferno.

Now here's where the story took an unexpected U-turn. Jim said, *"How 'bout we get together this week for lunch, but not to rehash anything you don't want to? You just may need a co-pastor friend about now."* I balked. I did say Jim was relentless, right? So that week we did lunch. It took Jim little time to ask me to teach an adult Sunday School class. *"What are you, nuts?"* again, not something I voiced. This I did say: *"Why would you wish to invite accusation against your church, given some of the stuff that has mushroomed well beyond reality?"* I told him, *"Let me decide first if this is where I should lock in. We'll put this on hold for now."*

By summertime, I was not only teaching Sunday School, Jim had asked me to lead a small group that met on Friday evenings. Wow! a mini-church! Soon thereafter, Jim even did the unthinkable: he asked me to cover the pulpit for him when he had scheduled a vacation. Then he did it again - and again. For the next five years, God had served me these three ministry platters. It was all good! I remain indebted to Jim for looking beyond the rumors and seeing the reclamation.

So, God was granting me a second chance to do what I love to do most, just not in the capacity I most loved doing it. But He also gave me my own "congregation" in the mental health field. Perhaps second chances translate into second best??? In this case, true.

Since that hinge moment in my life, God has ignited more than a few burning bushes. Each one transmits a redeeming message of second-chance love. What a comforting reminder to realize that despite my encore performances at failure, they can never outperform God's showers of Mercy!

I have renamed these second chances to align with our culture's 21st century skepticism. They are my "RCO's", my "Random Cosmic Occurrences". My recent life-path has intersected with more-than-a-few different people who raise their eyebrows in mock-pity for my *"blind trust"* in the Unverifiable. These individuals refuse to believe in a Personal Deity until He can pass the series of empirical tests that only *"sound science"* offers. I offer as my defense the recent parade of RCO's in my life that even caused them to pause and ponder. Now do these "testaments" of God prove His existence and the reasonableness of His Sovereign care for His Supposed Creation? No, but they sure seem to knock the stuffing out of the statistical probabilities to the contrary. I'll let you decide for yourself if these occurrences are as "random" and "cosmic" as today's prevailing evolutionary mindset presupposes. But first, allow me to prepare the soil of context before sharing my *"random"* episodes, for in doing so, it brings these two ideologies into starker contrast.

I had chosen, though I believe and therefore prefer to say, God had predestined, my career path. He had gifted me for pastoral ministry. So, I prepared myself via the usual means to that end, including three theological degrees. (More failure: all that wasted education! But I digress.) Before my marriage gasped its final breath, the church I had been serving rightfully requested my resignation. When it expired, I voluntarily stepped out of ministry altogether. Everything into which I had poured my heart and soul, including the investment of 13½ years of post high school education as well as the actual practice of 20+ years in the pastorate, swirled down the drain of Failure. At age 48, how do you start all over? Or how do you make the best of what you have with the amount of time left? What a quandary!!

But the God I serve awards second chances - despite us - despite me! And He employs RCO's to accomplish His restorative purposes. In my two realms of greatest failure, God embraced me with His "the-past-is-past" Mercy.

RCO Episode #1:

Despite our very small pool of shared assets, the divorce proceedings dragged on – and on. I cared little for material goods. I coveted sanity. The senior couple who were my surrogate grandparents, whom I affectionately called *"Grams and Gramps"*, gifted us a rocking chair for our wedding – one of a very few common property items I asked for. Though the divorce decree granted me that chair, I have yet to see it, much less rock in it. I guess I'll forever be *"off my rocker."*

Marriage had left a bad taste in my mouth. Was I attracted to other women before and after the ultimate fracture? I wasn't dead. BUT, I had little-to-no desire to get into any kind of relationship again. My coworkers and friends demonstrated far more interest in that matter than me. They were always trying to set me up.

There was one woman, however, I had determined to seek out who I hadn't seen in nearly 30 years! We had become friend's way back in college, and even dabbled at dating. The grapevine had done what it does second best (making wine is first): it revealed to me that her marriage too, had imploded. So, with three decades in both our rearview mirrors, and wondering if timing was now offering me a second chance, I reached out to her. We kinda picked up where we had left off. But as is often true that *"timing is everything,"* it wasn't for us; nothing came out of our reconnect. However, it did do this one thing for me: it aroused within me this glimmer of hope that I could potentially love again.

How could I ever forget that fortuitous day I first met this fervidly furious female in a fulsome frenzy - or was she a desperately distraught damsel in dire distress - with the Northern European accent? I had just gotten settled in my new office, working for another mental health provider. As in the prior two years, I would continue to provide counsel for troubled adolescents; I mean troubled. We speak of dysfunction so casually today; but what I witnessed day in and day out, stretched the definition to a whole new dimension. When I had been in the ministry, I had preached about man's depravity. In my new field, it smacked me in the face every day. Another overused word today is "victim"; everybody is a victim. But these kids gave definition to the term, with lifetime physical and emotional scars to prove it. I also got to meet their parents - if they were even in the picture. Often, they weren't. On my first day on the new job, I met one of those parents - or so I initially presumed.

This 40-something blond came storming into my office, screaming for the ear of my new coworker - whom she obviously knew, *"You won't believe what he did this time!"* I presumed she was one of the foster moms venting her exasperation over her foster kid's most recent transgression. I was wrong. I wasn't even close. She was one of the clinical staff. *("Oh, good grief! What have I gotten myself into?")* In fact, she was my new partner's old partner; which as I assessed the circumstance rather adroitly, I might add, meant she was the clinician I came to replace - and the clinician who would be training me. *("Lord, help me - find the nearest exit!")*

Sometimes the line between the mental health client and clinician is only separated by a volcanic episode in a person's life. It was the day after my new trainer's 48th birthday. What she received as a birthday gift the day before triggered her Vesuvian eruption.

For the next hour, plumes of ash spewed from that yellow crest and verbal-lava filled our cramped little office. It wasn't till later in the day that I realized I had changed wardrobes during the meltdown. I unconsciously shed my clinician's cloak to don my clergyman's collar. I sat. I listened. Occasionally I'd slip in an empathetic word of comfort or counsel. Over the ensuing weeks (my training went longer than anticipated; I am such a s l o w learner), I repeatedly pointed her to the God Who cared about her. She may not have been given a good gift on her birthday, but there was the best gift awaiting her any day she chose. Reflecting, she would often recite what rang familiar to Charles Dickens' immortal words: *"It was at once, one of the worst days of my life - and one of the best."*

That was back on April 22nd, 2002 when by the kismet of Random Cosmic Occurrence two confused and wounded people intersected at that critical moment in both of their lives. She was at her wit's end with heart-wrenching betrayal. I was at my wit's end with abject failure. Isn't this just like the karma of impersonal matter to sculpt so timely an event? Both my then-trainer and I think not. We share the conviction that this philosophy requires more faith than its converse. Accordingly, we believe in a Personal God Who Sovereignly rules from Heaven and orchestrates our every step on earth. We further believe He delights in arranging Divine appointments that bring hurting people He loves together for healing. And did we heal! so much so that on February 5th, 2005 *(carefully regard the date: 02-05 in 2005 at 2:05 in the afternoon. Chalk this up to my dogged OCD-perfectionism." For explanation, see the Diagnostic and Statistical Manual of Mental Disorders, Vol. 4.),* God presented both of us with His gift of a second chance. Mari and I wed.

Fast forward with a full decade now under our marital belt, we can look back and fully appreciate that God can take two broken people, and by extending to them His Inexhaustible Mercy, He will repair them. Oh, be assured, we still betray our innate dysfunction in bits and pieces every day. But we never cry out, *"Victim!"* We don't need to; because we possess this unshakable conviction that Jesus played that role for us when He died in our place 2,000 years ago, so we would never have to.

RCO Episode #2:

For seven interminable years, I had been divorced from the profession I loved. *(Whatever happened to seven being the "perfect" number?)* But it had to be this way because I had disqualified myself for spiritual leadership. I couldn't *"manage my own family"* at all, let alone *"well"*, so how could I *"take care of God's church?"* (see Bible: 1 Timothy 3:4-5) At least God had allowed me to taste the fresh fruit of His forgiveness in my remarriage. This helped me to accept that my years in ministry were behind me, at least the professional piece. God may have defrocked me, but He didn't strip me of His giftedness in my life. He kept filling my void with "small" (nothing is truly *small* in God's work) opportunities to minister. I had taught adult Sunday School classes and facilitated small group fellowships most of those less-than-best seven years. Not quite the same, but for me, an ego-salve. I didn't feel totally useless.

Meantime Mari was working as a clinical counselor. At the end of an otherwise innocuously normal workday, one of her coworkers knocked on her office door and introduced an RCO guest. Now most people sitting behind Mari's desk would've scratched their head in bewilderment when this complete stranger greeted them. Her words would've sounded like gibberish. But speaking Finnish to a Finn detonated this explosion of nostalgic delight! Mari hails from Finland. So, when her visitor greeted her in her native tongue, she leapt to her feet and into the arms of her new acquaintance. A friendship was born. Other staff listened to their exuberant exchange, but did not "hear". They heard the chatter, but could not understand the conversation; except enough to decipher that they had teleported to their shared motherland.

Over the next several weeks, the friendship blossomed. Then on one occasion as part of a typical casual conversation, Sirkka-Liisa said: *"Tell me about Bob."* So, Mari quickly painted this synoptic picture of who I was and what I did for a living. She wrapped up her brief bio with this otherwise-forgettable trivia tidbit: *"Although he too is in the mental health profession, his heart is still in the ministry."* Now this is something that Mari and I both knew, yet it was something we rarely shared openly. It hurt too much to pour salt on this perpetually-open wound. You can take the pastor out of the pastorate; but you can never take the pastorate out of the pastor.

The question was anything but *random* for it's one you'd expect as their relationship grew from acquaintance to friendship. But because it was so conventional, my wife had forgotten all about it ------- until one day, several months later, she received a call and heard the familiar voice of her Finnish friend. Sirkka-Liisa excitedly asked, *"Got a pen? You need to write down this number."* While Mari fetched a pen, her

Finn-friend continued unabated: *"I just got back from visiting a town I had never been in before* (random) *and picked up a local newspaper I had never seen before* (random) *and inexplicably turned to that section I never ever read because I am perfectly satisfied with my employment* (random); *I opened to the Classifieds. When I did, my eyes immediately lit upon this 2 x ½in. inset ad* (random) *that a church is looking for a part time pastor. Bob needs to apply."* Mari scribbled down the number as she scratched her head.

That evening, Mari's and my usual chit-chat got completely usurped by this twist-of-fate revelation. There was no repressing her inquisitive excitement over the prospect - knowing nothing about the particular church, much less the demands of ministry on the pastor's spouse. So, I immediately burst her spirited bubble by saying, *"You don't get how these things work. And aren't you forgetting I lost my qualification?"* Am I the only husband that doesn't like it when his wife denudes his holier-than-thou presumption with a simple rejoinder. She said, *"Can't we let God speak for Himself?"* OUCH!

Rather than swallowing my humble pie, my mind crafted how this needed to go: (*"I'll show her. I'll prove to her I'm disqualified. I'll call the church contact and jump through their application hoops. Then I'll lay out before my wife the search committee's short-and-sweet"* - make that *"terse-and-too-bad - form rejection letter."*) So, I launched into my plan - made the phone call and followed through with their directives. I waited impatiently because I was so eager to gloat. But time passed with nothing; not even the much-expected rejection letter. You'd think the church would at least have the decency to shoot me down rather than let me hang. *(Hmm. Either way, this doesn't sound very Christian.)*

Then after I had long presumed my application had made its way into the circular file, I received this much unanticipated phone call from the church's search committee. This must have been three to four months later and I had long dismissed this opening and went on with my mental-health-career life. They liked what they read in my resume. I wasn't surprised. Everyone's resume reads a whole lot better than the real deal. I looked pretty good on paper. Given just this, I'd even consider hiring me. Besides, who pads their resume with their delineation of failures? I may have been a failure, but I wasn't an idiot. So, this church had no clue what a screw-up I was. Nonetheless, the caller went on to explain their search process, but not before revealing to me that they had interest in three other candidates. They would conduct an in-person interview with each of us, followed by two pulpit opportunities. When I heard the word *"preach"*, my heart did a John-the-Baptist-in-the-womb leap. (See Bible: Luke 1:44) It began to pound for the chance to be back in the homiletical saddle. But I knew better than to allow my emotions to run unbridled. So, I planned to assure my rejection. Failures fail, right? So, I might as well plan to fail. (Spare yourself trying to figure this out.) But at the interview, I'd unveil my plural failures, beginning with my marital failure and climaxing with my ministerial failure. Then I would preach two very ordinary sermons, consciously choosing not to give them two of my best shots (this would be simple enough as all my sermons hovered around the level of mediocrity). Since I was good at failure, why not fail really good!

During my interview, the search committee informed me regarding the church's timeframe for calling the vote. So at least I knew when to expect the rejection. Once all four candidates had completed their fair-and-equal opportunity, the church members would cast their secret ballot; after which time I would condescendingly announce to my wife, *"I told you so."*

On the anticipated date, I didn't have to wait long. My heart played hopscotch all the way to the phone, and not for the reason you may presume. Buried deep within the covetous corner of my heart, I desperately longed to be back doing what God had gifted me to do; even if just part time in a very small church of 35 folks! I had prepared my mind for the rejection; but I had forgotten to have that same dialogue with my heart. It had sunken somewhere into my gastrointestinal tract, elevating nausea up into my throat.

Some phone calls you never forget. This was one of them. My caller, having identified himself as G.T., started out by saying, *"I want to be the first to congratulate you for being selected as the next pastor of Lighthouse Reformed Church."* I should have been thrilled, even considering I had to take another bite out of my humble pie when my wife could instead say to me, *"I told you so."* *"What is wrong with me?"* I needed more; more convincing evidence that this was God's vote, not man's. But of course, other than the Lord Himself, nobody knew the torturous game my mind was playing. But because He did (Random Cosmic Occurrence? Nah!), and knowing what my insecurity needed at that moment, these words broke through my silent musings: *"And for the first time ever in our 100-year history,* (the church had just celebrated their 100th birthday the month prior) *we had a unanimous vote."*

(*"Did I just hear, right? Really? You mean, God, You're really giving me a second chance at ministry???"*) As soon as I placed the receiver on its cradle, tears gushed - and gushed - and gushed. Seven years of pent-up emotional self-flagellation came like a tsunami. My wife embraced me and together we cried. If she ever toyed with the temptation to say, *"I told you so"*, she never betrayed a trace. God, on the other Hand, did: *"If I gave Moses, Jonah and Peter second chances, why did you ever doubt that in My Mercy and Grace I might do the same for you? I told you so!"* The tears started Round 2.

For the ensuing 13 months, I lived a foretaste of Heaven again. I can't find adequate words to match my heart's elation. I so loved being back in the ministry. I'll say it again: I so loved being back in the ministry. Even better, I so loved feeling loved by the Paragon of Love. For three decades I had preached Grace. Now I realized what it was to receive a blessing I didn't deserve. For three decades I had preached Mercy. Now I knew what that really meant to be spared a consequence I did deserve. For three decades, I had preached Forgiveness. Now I felt fully immersed in it and washed by it. God *"told me so"*. My heart finally caught up to my head.

But God wasn't done with His outpouring of Mercy-and-Grace-on-me yet.

RCO Episode #3:

Mari discovered she loved the pastorate as much as me; notwithstanding that I had forewarned her about the pressures ministry places on marriages. But our part time experience seemed to defy everything I had projected. It also triggered an even deeper yearning in my spirit to be back in fulltime ministry. How could I be so audacious as to assume that God would open this door for this failure-twice-over? My wife sensed my restlessness. She suggested we make this a matter of prayer. I dared not try to "correct" her thinking this time.

Why is it that we often pray in faith, yet take it upon ourselves to help God with its answer? Now I know the tension that exists between *"waiting on God"*, both in the praying piece and in the pausing piece, and in the *"faith without works is dead"* piece. I know God opens and shuts doors, but how much of the walking up the sidewalk and knocking on the door is our duty? Well my bride and I made our decision in this case.

Now Mari and I may have misinterpreted God's Plan at this point, or had vainly presumed we could expand it for Him; but we were thinking rationally here: How can you effectively grow a ministry when you live an hour and a half away from the church? That's right. This little assembly of Christians we had been pastoring for the past several months was a 50+ mile commute. Here's that tension-enigma thing again: It's the Holy Spirit Who grows churches, but He uses people to do the work. So, we thought we should start knocking on doors in the town we'd been serving. We contacted a realtor and began house hunting.

For two months in the summer of 2008, we had diligently searched - while continuing to pray. We saw some very nice homes; in fact, one was an exact model of the home in which we had been residing, only smaller. We contemplated our next move. Now some of you will identify with this: Because we didn't sense God's peace blanketing our hearts, experience had taught us to slow things down. We put our *"knocking"* on hold.

I don't remember the exact date, but I know it was right around Halloween when the urge to *"knock"* again swept over us. We had *"waited on the Lord"* - and were convinced we had waited long enough. But looking back, our action looked more like Abraham and Sarah of old who knew the Promise of a son was in the making, so they helped God - along with Hagar - to make it happen. (See Bible: Genesis 16:1-16) We even modified our recurrent prayer to echo the *"prayer of Jabez"*. (See Bible: 1 Chronicles 4:9-10) From that moment, Mari fully trusted that we were knocking at Heaven's Door and God would soon delight us with His next "Treat". Meanwhile, the negative me was hoping-against-hope that my ego - or the demonic realm - wasn't playing on me some nasty "Trick".

In our first Jabez-prayer, I had requested in concert with the historical *"Jabez"* of the Old Testament, *"Would You, Father, out of Your Mercy and Grace 'enlarge [our] border?'"* Now by this we did not mean we were asking for a larger home or property. Instead we simply meant, *"Please Lord, open a door for us in fulltime ministry."*

Why would our spirits now be so persuaded to move unless God was in this? We had prayed. We had waited. We had peace, while faithfully serving throughout. So now, this must be His Will. We reconnected with our realtor. We asked her if the same three houses we liked from our summer search were still on the market? No, enlarging our border did not mean purchasing all three. But yes, all three were still on the market. She arranged a mid-November Sunday afternoon when we'd already be out in the vicinity for the worship service. We looked at the home we most liked, the dwarf-twin of our home. Oh, and the best part, it sat but a *"hop without a skip and a jump"* down the street from the church! *Double Random Cosmic Occurrence!* - a match and a stroll. We were ready to move on it and said to her, *"We'll put in an offer next Sunday when we come back out here."* We were in no hurry. But we wanted to pray a little more - just to be "sure". Besides, it had been on the market for almost 17 months.

Our realtor called us on Friday of that week and said, *"A full price offer was just made on the house today; and I'm sure the owner is going to accept it."* Wow. Didn't see that one coming. *("Really God?")* But at least the other two houses were still on the market; one having been listed for 9 months, the other for 13. She said she would arrange another walk-through with our 2nd choice the following Sunday. A tad disheartened from our 1st choice now off the board, we weakly replied, *"OK,"* still reeling from the perplexing disappointment. But we clung to our conviction that God was in control - is in control - and we knew that He knew the Jabez that was best suited for us. Realigning our wills to conform to His, however, when all the "signs" pointed to the house that mirrored ours on the street just one block from the church that unanimously called us to serve, left us befuddled.

The following Sunday we met the realtor at the second house. We liked it, though from our human yen, it wasn't the match the first was. But we were here to serve and *"enlarge our border"*. A house is a house. We said we'll pray on it and if it *"still feels right"* by next Sunday (meaning if we sustain God's peace throughout the week), we'll put a bid on it.

The realtor called us midweek and said, *"You won't believe this, but someone made a bid on the house."*

("Really God? Twice! Is this my punishment for failing in both my former marriage and ministry??") Negative, I know.

I barely heard her continue with her offer to take another walk-through of the third house, but *"not next Sunday because I have a prior commitment for the Thanksgiving weekend. I can meet the first Sunday of December."* Our emotional sails felt very little Holy Spirit wind behind them at this news. Nonetheless, we agreed to go and give it "one last"(?) shot.

With just a few days remaining before we went to look at the third house, I saw the realtor's number light up on our phone. I remember the tumultuous storm in my gut. I prayed that she was merely confirming our scheduled appointment. Her first words didn't register at first: *"Could we hire you?"*

"What?" I retorted.

She elaborated, *"Every time you show interest in a house, it sells that week. Might you have any interest in any of our other homes we've currently got listed? We'll pay you 10% of closing costs."* Funny - but not.

Our drive home that Sunday afternoon was deafeningly quiet. My mind battled with trying to make some sense out of all that had transpired over the past month. Three homes, all on the market for several months, and each bought out from underneath us in the very week we were poised to put bids on them! I had misread this string of *Random Cosmic Occurrences.* You see I had been silently suspecting all along that Satan would sabotage my aspiration to get back into fulltime ministry. But this was way too random for even Satan. This was clearly God's doing! Yeah, He must have still harbored at least some degree of anger against me for my two big failures.

If only I had pondered biblically as opposed to egocentrically, the Holy Spirit would've been granted some room to operate inside my cluttered mind. Only later did I recall that account in Acts 16 where the

Apostle Paul had every intention of entering Asia to promote the Gospel, but as the text puts it, *"because the Holy Spirit had prevented them from preaching the word in the province of Asia"*. It's not that God didn't care about the Asians, or the central Pennsylvanians, but He did have plans for Europe and a small municipality in eastern PA. In fact, had it not been God's redirecting Paul to enter Europe, the Gospel may never have come to anywhere in Pennsylvania, let alone the somewhat tiny town of Nazareth. And I'd probably be a rice farmer.

Mari and I had been traveling the 65-mph speed limit eastbound on Route 80 for about a half hour when I raised both of my arms. No, I was not caught up in some charismatic flash of euphoric worship. And yes, there was now no direct linkage between my hands and the steering wheel. I know what you're thinking, *"You'd lost it. You've come unhinged."* You'll be even more convinced I had *"skipped out"* when you hear that we continued down the highway in that fashion for the next near-mile?! Really. No knees either, guiding the wheel. *(Not recommended for modeling faith. Thankfully the road was straight, and my tires aligned. And please, don't ask me about my wife. I can't remember what she was doing, now down on the floor of the car. Out of the corner of my eye, I could see ever-burgeoning traces of sheer terror. She remained conspicuously silent though. Was it because she knew I was emotionally drained or because she learned the meaning of "scared stiff?" I suspect she was praying more fervently than she ever had before - her white knuckles betraying her intensity.)*

I shattered the silence. *"What are You telling me, Father? Have I disqualified myself from full time service? You know me better than I know me. So, You already know that all I want to do is serve You and Your Kingdom Cause."* The remainder of my vertical conversation took place within the private confines of my convoluted mind - though I couldn't help but echo - and personalize - President Franklin D. Roosevelt's immortal words on this the 67th anniversary of Japan's invasion of Pearl Harbor: *"Today is a date which will live in my infamy."* For the world incomparably and immeasurably more; but for me on this day, a microcosmic implosion.

As we drove the homestretch - I can even see the exact place in my mind's eye - we passed a new store front church (funny - but not). Sighing deeply, I acquiesced. *"Father, if all I ever get to do for the rest of my life is part time ministry, it'll be far more than I ever deserve. And I will be content with that."* Confessedly, my heart still needed to catch up with my head. It took the next full week to do so.

On Sunday evening, December 21st, having preached a Christmas message earlier in the day in the church that I would faithfully serve part time for as long as God orchestrated, I went to bed early. Was I just simply tired, or spiritually wearied by our vain search to relocate and assist God in *"enlarging our border"*? I instructed Mari, *"If anyone calls for me, tell them I'll get in touch with them sometime tomorrow."* I hadn't been in bed but five minutes. I can still picture the clock at 9:05pm when the phone rang. By my wife's response, I knew it was for me. Though I possessed no clue who was on the other end of the line, I could reconstruct some of the exchange. The excitement in my wife's voice, as betrayed by her very LOUD Q & A's, coupled with the fact that she had conversed with someone she didn't even know for a full hour, I deduced it had to do with the church we attended before relocating to central Pennsylvania.

I give Mari tremendous credit for sustaining restraint from calling me to the phone as per my request. But I can't afford her the same credit when she hung up the receiver. She raced into our bedroom the second she hung up to excitedly retell the recent exchange. She began by saying that the caller didn't even identify himself at first, but instead spouted, *"Hallelujah! I got the right Hampton's."* What was that all about? As the unknown-to-me-as-yet caller had explained to Mari, he had been scanning through the White Pages in the hope of locating us.

All he had remembered was central PA - and that was three years ago. He had no idea if we had relocated again. He wasn't surprised to see nearly a column of Hamptons listed - and several *"fit"* with either *B., R., Bob, Rob or Robert*. Relying partly on logic, but mostly on *Random*, he dialed one of the many options. Admittedly, this wasn't a full *RCO*, but it was at least a partial one. Our caller knew he had hit pay dirt the second Mari answered the phone in her characteristic way, *"Hello, who's calling please?"* But it wasn't because of what she had said that had elicited his spontaneous eruption; it was because of how she sounds. Her distinctive Finnish accent is a dead giveaway every time. She needn't ever identify herself saying, *"Hello, this is Mari"*. Yes, the other party was Rick from our church of three years ago, back in eastern Pennsylvania. (I've often chuckled over that evening and wondered what his first words might have been if *Random* had dialed him through a string of *"wrong Hampton's."* *"Sorry, I'm looking for the right Hampton's! You're obviously wrong."* That probably would not have been received too well. But it would've been funny.)

Was I grateful that Mari had honored the *"letter"* of my request by not disturbing me during the call, but missed the *"spirit"* of my request by disturbing me afterwards? For the sleep I had so coveted, eluded me as her effervescent voice kept scaling new decibel levels on the phone. And any hope of sleep when she had hung up, wasn't going to happen. She flew up the stairs, catapulted herself atop the bed and proceeded to clone the prior hour's entire conversation! I would have much preferred the Reader's Digest version; better yet, Cliff's Notes.

In the morning, I followed up the prior night's phone call as per Rick's request, dialing one of the church's elders. He explained to me that the pastor resigned the prior morning and they needed some help. *"OK, what would you like me to do? Recommend an interim or provide some counsel to persons wounded from whatever transpired?"* I had been in the field too many years to know that there's always hurt and grief in the departure of a pastor, even under good circumstances. And these circumstances sounded far less than good. The elder responded, *"Not exactly. Would you come to be our pastor?"* Had I heard that right? I asked for reiteration. I had heard it right.

God had granted me a second, second chance! *"Full time?? Really?? Me, the big-time failure??"*

There was a catch. *("I knew it. Here it comes.")* I soon learned how depleted the membership had become; which translates into a near empty coffer. This elder did assure me that my check would be the first one written each week; but it could bounce quite high. *"That's the catch?? That's no catch. I had told God - and His people - many times, I'd do this for free!"*

So, I made a counteroffer: *"If you permit me to keep my current employment until the church gets financially solvent again, I will provide leadership, counseling and preaching on the weekends."* I couldn't see through the phone, but I believe this 50-something year old elder did a back flip - at least partially. *"A free pastor!"*

Well free to the church, but I was still being compensated. I chuckled inwardly with this twist of Divine irony: a secular organization paying the freight for my new sectarian work. It gave a whole new meaning to the non-separation of church and state. So, God had met our needs, as we knew He would: *"My God will meet all of your needs according to His riches in Christ Jesus"* (Philippians 4:19). But truth be told, my faith here resided less in trusting God to meet our needs and more in sustaining my current employment. May I pass on a word of counsel at this juncture? Be very careful the noble, yet vacuous assertions you make; for God may hold you to them. *"I'd do this for free!"* I'd often - boast??? But I'd always say this with at least one safety net to catch me if circumstances changed. And that's what I had here - a safety net of fulltime employment. But it's at times like these, God delights in prodding us to trust Him all the more. So, to ensure I

45

would do just this and not rely on my safety net, He yanked it out from under me. He wasn't being mean; He was holding me accountable for a claim that may have been more pious than honest. It's too easy to make sanctimonious assertions when there's no true risk involved. I suspect an analysis of such claims find their greater motivation tucked somewhere in our subliminal craving to impress our fellow man as opposed to sincerely aspiring to live a life of full-scale faith in God. Just three weeks after I had accepted this unsalaried full-time position, the company for which I had faithfully worked for 7 years, downsized me. *(That's the preferred term today, right?? I got canned, released, sent packing, fired.)*

I initiated the ensuing dialogue. *"Are You sure You know what You're doing, God? The church is near broke, I'm now unemployed; and like everybody else, I've got bills to pay."* Did I really think I was enlightening the Omniscient God with some facts that somehow slipped past His Omnipresent Eye? Why do we sometimes converse with Him as though He's taken a potty break? Well His response reminded me that nothing slips through the cracks of innocuous living. Though inaudible, I heard His *"I'm holding-your-feet-to-the-fire"* retort: *"You've always said you'd do this for free. Just making sure you meant it. Holding you accountable. Besides, and more important, I'm refining your character through the whole 'Trust-Me-completely' factor of sanctifying faith."*

Now I'm backpedaling. *"Lord, I've had enough character-development over the past decade to last me a lifetime. And as for the ministry-for-free thing, You know that from day one when I launched out into ministry, I never, ever, not even once, requested either a salary range or a raise. Certainly, You're taking into account this noble track record for 'being content with whatever you have'.* (See Bible: Philippians 4:11) *Doesn't this count for something?!"*

Then His Holy Spirit gently reminded me that the life of faith resides under His canopy of Grace, that no compilation of good works on my part - our part - merits special consideration. *"So, are you going to trust Me and only Me or are you going to try to argue your lame case that retains a built-in safety net?"*

In the days that followed as I plodded forward through the church's constitutional protocol to move from invitation to installation, the Holy Spirit performed some serious soul-cleaning on me. Somehow, I had gotten sidetracked from the answered Jabez-prayer that God had reopened the door to fulltime ministry for me. Instead I was murmuring over my unexpected fiscal freefall, failing to practice everything I had ever preached about faith.

Another *random* phone call marked a pivotal change in my perspective. With the myriad of phone calls we receive in a lifetime, many we forget and some we can recall the gist. This one I can virtually regurgitate the entire, howbeit brief, conversation. At age 55 and my wife not trailing far behind at 54, I assure you, we were not looking to *"enlarge her belt border"*. Besides, barring Divine intervention in the likeness of Abraham and Sarah, biology had shut and locked the door on our fertility. So, when Paula, one of my wife's coworkers, announced, *"Mari just went into labor"*, I knew this had nothing to do with a pregnancy that I had somehow missed over the past nine months. Without even a momentary lapse, I blurted out, *"Dear Lord, she's bringing home another puppy!"* Not many people, not even married people, would have so instantly connected these dots. But I knew my wife's love for dogs - all animals for that matter - save snakes and bats (especially bats, as one had bitten her in the eye. Yep, she needed that series of rabies injections to the midsection. Not fun at all; but what a trooper! She never *bat*-ted an eye.) It bumps right up near her love for children. *("Really Honey, we already have two dogs!")* But I'm an easy mark. So, after the shortest pregnancy and easiest delivery ever, we expanded our rescued "offspring" of two Toy Poodles, one male, one female. Mari brought home from her workplace this rejected, runt-of-the-litter, Teacup Chihuahua; though a Prince in his own mind (who has never let us, or anyone else, ever forget it).

Now what do we name him? We don't. For God's epiphany in the timing of this other and far-lesser Prince limited our choice to but one name. God couldn't have wisped the clouds into letters of keener legibility. His name would be *"Jabez"*. During that small window of waiting to confirm our calling, God sealed the deal through a forsaken puppy; the puppy bred for show, but denied from show, because like his new owner, he had failed in his qualification.

Jabez has been a part (he would contend the main and central part) of our home for eight years now, during which time, my wife and I have discovered two very practical benefits arising from his chosen name. First, when he's in a crowd of dogs and we call his name, we never fear a stampede. And second, when people ask his name, it affords us the privilege to launch into our story of how the God we serve answers second-chance prayers.

Was it really *random* that three house doors, long open, closed abruptly? Was it really *random* that at the point of my greatest exasperation, a phone call transformed everything into exhilaration? Was it really *random* that another phone call gave birth to more than a dog? Yep. That's the *Random* God I worship - only I spell *random, S-o-v-e-r-e-i-g-n!*

Chapter 4
Failure under God - A Miracle in the Making

The entire time I sat on the sideline of the pastorate, I felt like a former starfish amputee (I'm leaping to the assumption that starfish have feelings), which having lost one of its "arms", regenerates a new one in its place. I now floated atop the celestial clouds of forgiveness and second chances while basking in the light of restored ministry. Back into fulltime, professional Christian ministry! I was one restored and fulfilled starfish.

Confirmations of my restoration came in different shapes and sizes; but one of the best came in the shape of an old farm house of 1700 square feet. Mari and I now understood why three house deals fell through the year prior; we were looking west while God was calling us east.

Mari and I like old houses; there's something about the aura surrounding a century's old house. We checked out several younger homes, but they weren't us. Neither were their price tags. But even the few that fell below our agreed-upon cap cost, didn't lure us away from our penchant for an older home. One day our realtor told us of a house that fit our hopes. It even set on a one+-acre plot of land with beautifully-sculpted gardens, an above-ground pool and an oval gazebo! We loved it - inside and out! - except for the price tag. Even with some wiggle room to negotiate, there was still no way. Besides, there were seven other moderate-to-strong interested parties. Bummer.

I set aside my emotions to let it go; which didn't work too well. I would have preferred we never saw the place because seeing and not getting became torturous. I didn't sleep well that night. But Mari did. Evidently, I liked the place more - or so I thought. The following morning, she instructed me that we're to call the realtor and place a bid - are you ready for this? - at the price God told her in a dream to offer.

Immediately I grew suspect that either her prescription drug effected an adverse reaction, or she had eaten too much pepperoni pizza the night before. She shared the figure. Yep, either the medication or the pizza - or both. She stated a price $25K below the basement of the wiggle room. I responded, *"Mari, that's insulting. I can't go to our realtor with that number."* She insisted. I acquiesced. He responded, *"That's insulting. I can't go to the owner's realtor with that figure."* Seriously, he employed the very same adjective I had. I attempted to explain, *"Mari said that God said this is the offer we're to make."* I think I saw his eyes roll; but who would want to chance disagreeing with God - or worse, with Mari? So, after a few gentle pleas, he agreed to place the bid; though he added we should expect a denial.

Our realtor met with the other realtor and shared our offer, but prepped him for it by saying, *"I have an offer from the Hamptons. It's low, but they did build in a little wiggle room."* He barely spoke our offer when his counterpart fired back, *"That's insulting."* At least there was this agreement across the board.

Our realtor somehow convinced his competitor to submit the offer. He met with the owner later that afternoon, stating, *"We have an offer, but it's very low."* Now what should have been the logical follow-up question from the owner, *"How low?"* was never spoken. Keep in mind, there were eight interested parties, which is why the owner's counter question was so unexpected, *"Was the offer made by the Hampton's?"* Very odd question to ask, especially in that she didn't know us from Adam and Eve; well maybe from Adam and Eve.

Baffled by the non-sequitur question, the realtor, shrugging his shoulders, simply answered, *"Well as a matter of fact."*

Now if the owner's question didn't blindside the realtor, her subsequent declaration most certainly did. *"It's theirs."*

OK, something got lost in the transmission. Obviously, she had a pre-senior senior moment. She couldn't have heard her realtor accurately. So as though groping for what to say next, the realtor puzzledly asked, *"Well don't you want to know how much they're offering?"*

"Doesn't matter. I want them to have my house." I confess, I'm still not much of a *"God-spoke-to-me-in-a-dream kind of guy,"* but I strongly believe that *"God's Ways are Higher than our ways."* (see Bible: Isaiah 55:8-9) In this case, His High Way opened the door, literally, to our driveway and house and yard. Just one more confirmation that God had restored me to the pastorate.

God had sprinkled a few additional confirmations that helped me sense His Pleasure in restoring me to fulltime pastoral ministry. But none of these confirmations spoke louder to me than this one: I was still breathing. I sense your ambivalence. *"How does breathing confirm placement? All it confirms is life."* Exactly. And without life, it's profoundly difficult to minister - even part time.

My Heart Wasn't in It

Yes, I was still breathing - but not like I used to. Something had changed within me only after two years in that former ministry. I began to feel easily winded. On three separate occasions within a relatively short timeframe, I huffed and puffed during rather casual exercise. The first one occurred on an unseasonably mild January day. Not an avid jogger, but one who enjoys an occasional lope, I decided to capitalize on the spring-teaser. A half mile into my run, I couldn't get "over the wall", a phrase familiar to runners. I couldn't transition from the lactic acid stage of running when you feel that burn in the legs to the oxygen stage when you feel like you can sprint a marathon. A mile into my run and I felt like I had lost all my breath to catch. But I hadn't exercised much since the fall. So, I wrote this off as just one more annoying symptom of stepping closer to the threshold of my seasoned years (a.k.a. senior years).

The second "event" hurt my pride. I was hanging out with several of the church teens in our all-purpose room. One of the young men, dribbling a basketball, challenged me to a game of one-on-one. How could I decline such an ego-booster? Now normally, I would've whooped his tail. *(OK, probably not.)* But on this occasion, just 30 seconds into the match, I was gasping for air. Fortunately for my pride, the Youth Pastor called his meeting to order and my contest was cut short. I over-exaggerated how winded I was by saying something to this teen like, *"Man, you've gotten good. What are you trying to do to this old man?"* Meantime, I wasn't nearly as concerned about my pride for having lost as I was about having confirmed my senior status.

It was the third "event", however, that triggered my decision to call my doctor. I was coming to terms that perhaps I had some medical anomaly going on. I didn't wish to alarm Mari though. So, I asked her if we could go for a spirited walk at the local park. Because she loves getting outdoors and doing something physical, she was all over this request. We would do this once or twice per week, taking all three of our dogs in tow. They loved these strolls even more than she did. So, this was nothing that could alarm her, not even when I requested she bring along a cell phone. In fact, she interpreted this as my tendency to blur the line between family and work time. So immediately she said - and rightly so - *"No, the church can live without you for an hour; the phone stays home!"* Hmm - problem. How do I convince her that we better have a phone handy in the event I pass out? Coupled with my shortness of breath lately, I had grown increasingly dizzy. We started our walk, and at a better-than-moderate clip - my doing - until we came to a rather steep and protracted incline. I don't think we made 100 feet into that climb when Mari turned to ask me a question. Actually, she turned to nobody, as I wasn't there. She turned around to look back down the trail and there I stood – sort'a - half bent over, hands on my knees. No, I wasn't praying. She raced to my side and said, *"Okay, what's going on?"* I told her I had no clue; but whatever it was, it had been going on for at least four months now.

We headed right home and called our primary care doc. She told us to come right over. After some preliminary analysis, she said I had likely developed an adult onset of asthma. *("Great.")* So, she put me on a daily protocol of oral steroids. Now I'm no medical expert, but I knew the difference between human lungs and water balloons; though in my case, they seemed to bear an uncanny resemblance. I returned to her office two weeks later, following my perfectionist bent to do everything I was told to do after my first visit; despite the fact I was near-drowning in my own phlegm. Her next diagnosis blindsided me: *"I'm going to send you to a cardiologist".*

("Beg your pardon? "What does my heart have to do with anything? It's my lungs that can't breathe.") I didn't know how interrelated they were; except of course, when you're in love: the heart skips while your breath is taken away.

So, in mid-spring of 2011, I added one more specialist to my ever-growing list of medical experts. I was already *seeing* an ophthalmologist - but barely as I had torn the retina in my left eye. I was also frequenting an orthopedic, an osteopathic and a neurologic doctor for my degenerative, herniated and ruptured L5 and S1 discs, as well as for a torn right rotator cuff; a dermatologist for facial and back squamous cells; an oral surgeon for a degenerative jawbone and diseased dental roots from a long-past car accident when I had lost 11 teeth to a Chevy Corvair dashboard; a gastroenterologist for acid reflux; a psychologist for depression; and an urologist and a proctologist for - well, you know.

Because of the prevalence of heart attacks in our stress-saturated culture, its warning signs are common knowledge: chest pain or pressure, an elevated heart rate, jaw pain, a dull ache radiating down the left arm, nausea, dizziness, sweating and/or sweaty palms, a clammy feeling and shortness of breath. Excepting for the last one, and an occasional sense of lightheadedness, I exhibited none of the other symptoms. Nevertheless, he ordered I take a stress test. I passed, though not with flying colors; but plenty good to allay any fears - except with the doctor. He next ordered a nuclear stress test, explaining that my genetic predisposition warranted such. Both of my grandfathers had died from cardiac infarction in their mid-50's, my mom had two heart attacks in her senior years and my physically-fit kid brother suffered two arrests (not criminal) by the time he turned 50!

Mari and I were sitting side-by-side on a hospital gurney, giving little thought of the outcome. I felt too good to have a problem. But as my cardiologist approached us, having just read my test report, we could see in his face that betraying look of less-than-good-news. I spoke first, *"This isn't good, is it?"*

"Not good at all", came his prompt reply.

Mari needed facts, so she immediately interjected, *"How bad is it?"*

The doctor's answer was not likely one he learned in medical school ethics, but at least we got the answer we sought - not the answer we wanted, but the answer we needed. *"How would you like to wake up next to a dead man?"* She turned to me and inquired about whether my life insurance payments were current. Kidding.

She blanched, and I logically asked, *"So what does this mean? Angioplasty? Stents?"*

He furrowed his brows and grimaced in such a way that inaudibly said, *"You're kidding, right?"* His verbal comeback cut to the chase. Soon it would cut through my chest. *"Surgery. You need a triple by-pass where we slice through your chest, split your rib cage wide apart, excise your heart from its sanctuary* (no, it doesn't really leave the chest; merely gets manhandled and rewired)*, place it in this machine for a lube job, cut into your leg and extract somewhere between 18 and 34 inches of vein and then perform some rewiring wizardry on the* *arterial vessels surrounding your heart. And if things go well, we'll put your heart back where it belongs."*

The rest of the conversation got blurred by the fog that enveloped my brain. I do remember asking the obvious, *"When will this happen?"*

He enlightened us with, *"Well, we'd love to take you into the OR right now, but we can't. Your arteries are feasting on nuclear dye. So, if you were to code while lying on the operating table, and we applied the paddles, you would fry from the inside out."* He attempted to give us a visual of what that would look like, explaining, *"Picture a toaster oven in your chest cavity. Then it shorts. In a flash, you'd be toast, literally - from the inside out."* Neither my wife nor I found this revelation very appealing - especially me. I'd been burned by others in the past, but never by a doctor, and most assuredly, not with such finality.

So, I proceeded with, *"Well when then?"*

Stoically the doctor spelled out the anticipated chronology. *"The nuclear material needs 48 hours to clear. So, first thing Monday morning, you're on."*

I sheepishly asked, *"Do I have a choice?"*

"Of course, you do," he answered matter-of-factly; just before he added, *"But I can't guarantee you'll be alive come Monday morning."* He proceeded to unveil the gravity of my condition. *"You have four major blockages of your three main arteries leading from your heart. The best one is 92% clogged. The others are 95%, 97% and one completely clogged at 100%. Your immediate future is uncertain, but I can tell you this: you're already on borrowed time."* Then turning to face Mari, he flatly stated, *"I assure you, he won't be around to celebrate Christmas."* Given the perspective of the whole, surgery began to sound like a real inviting option. I never thought I'd so look forward to having my rib cage sawed asunder and my heart yanked out of its nest.

Mari and I staggered from the hospital office, barely speaking a word except within the safe recesses of our own minds. I could see she was wrestling with the ominous forecast even more than I. I knew I needed to take the initiative here and steer this rather dark turn of events towards some glimmer of light. So, as we slogged our way up this unforgiving incline to retrieve our car from the parking lot, I deemed it a good idea to gasp, grab my chest and slump over. Mari freaked - but not near as much as when I stood tall and said, *"Gotcha'."* I didn't need to worry about the outcome of Monday's surgery; I had to first survive my unscheduled head trauma surgery. At least I didn't have to be transported very far. Because of my brush with murder by reason of momentary insanity, I've applied for a patent to be printed on every marriage license to read: *"Warning to husbands: The Surgeon General has determined that a little levity insufficiently weighed prior to implementation may prove hazardous to your health."*

Sleeping the next two nights proved difficult. Was it because of the anxiety over my uncertain future? Or was it the glow from the nuclear dye that lit up our bedroom?

My new best friend, the cardiologist, bumped me up to Number 1 on the surgical docket Monday morn. They admitted me at 5am, prepped me for the OR and asked me if I had any final words. (I knew what he meant, but he may want to rethink how to couch this request with future patients.) With the surgical team gathered all around my gurney, I spoke in a blanket of peace, *"I'm great. How can I not be? I'm in an all-win situation. If I wake up on this side of life, my eyes will light upon the beauty of my bride, Mari. If I wake up on the other side of life, my eyes will light upon the Beauty of my Groom, Jesus."* Several puzzled looks stared back at me, while furtive glances ricocheted between the cardiac care team members. Quickly they administered the anesthesia.

The next ten hours flew by - for me. I hadn't enjoyed so sound sleep in years. But for Mari, they were ten excruciating hours, including occasional updates from the surgeon. She sat in the OR waiting room with a few others in her circumstance, but nobody else for nearly as long. Aside from occasional chit-chat, they usually just sat numbed and mute, deep in their personal thoughts. A phone served as their lifeline to the OR, and they all desperately wanted it to ring with good news. Funny that they all sat in eager anticipation, but the moment it rang, they just sat still with a look of dread - each time. An undeniable flash of panic on each one's face betrayed their frazzled emotions. Several calls had come in over the first three and a half hours of trepidation, when finally, the caller asked for Mrs. Hampton. I know the doctor intended his words to be comforting, but how could they be? *"We've just opened up your husband's chest cavity and removed his heart. It's in the bypass machine as we speak."* Now you gain this clear sense that Mari's mind was bouncing all over the anxiety spectrum because she responded to the caller, pleading: *"Please don't drop it."* Glad I hadn't heard that.

In stark contrast, as previously noted, those ten hours traveled like the speed of light for me. One nanosecond I had closed my eyes in peaceful repose, and the next I had opened them up in the bliss of heavy medication. My eyes lit upon my bride and not even the sedation could mask or mar her beauty. The day went exceptionally well - for me - until then.

Evidently God had more for me to do here. That's what my mind filtered as I lay in the recovery room with needles and tubes hooked up to my every natural portal and then some manmade ones too. But this thought quickly evaporated when I reached the critical care room. There were several other patients sharing that singular room where we could all receive constant surveillance as we recovered from the day's invasive trauma. All the others were sleeping peacefully. Not me. My surgical resume, though brief, reports that I fight off anesthesia - and quite effectively. Twice (out of a total of only four) I've awoken in the middle of surgeries. On one of those occasions, I shocked the doc when I uttered, *"Are you just about done stitching me up? It's starting to really hurt."* If the anesthesia outlasts me, I always wake up as soon as I arrive in recovery.

So, there I lay awake in the confines of my own musings; everyone else sound in their slumber. Then something happened I had only wished was the hallucinatory effects of my sedation. Another of the patients awoke; and more than awoke. The moment she gained a modicum of lucidity, she went berserk. Seeing all these tubes sticking in and out of her, she began ripping them out. She then threw herself off the hospital bed and scrambled to her feet – kinda. She grabbed the first surgical tool within reach and started flailing and stumbling all over the place. What irony! I had just survived a major operation, only to fall victim to the frenzied eruption of another patient who went ballistic. Aides and nurses poured into the room in breakneck speed and did their heroic best to save her and everyone else around her. Double irony! I'm the only other patient awake, and I could see all this mayhem unfolding before me. I don't know how long this chase and capture took, probably less than a minute, but I can tell you, the posse had one heck of a time capping this volcano. I know what you're thinking, but no, I was not experiencing some psychotropic-induced hallucination. For throughout the night, the nursing staff kept asking if I was okay. They were obviously concerned over my emotional state as I was physically recuperating. I felt like saying, *"Yea, I'm fine. I had my heart torn from my chest earlier in the day and I just finished watching a drug-induced lunatic going manic in Recovery. Yea, just great!"* No doubt they were equally – or more – concerned over my mental state in our litigious culture. I had never been so pampered – though a back massage and steak dinner were out of the question. I had asked.

Add here a triple irony. I was being discharged on the Friday after my Monday surgery. I had bounced back incredibly well, surpassing every marker that signals when a patient is safe to go home. The entire cardiac team had gathered in my room as my nurse was spelling out my discharge duties. The lead doctor then asked me if I had any concerns or final questions. Sheepishly, I nodded. I did have one concern that had been plaguing me from the moment I had learned I required surgery; but a little surgical history here is in order. I had only two prior surgeries as an adult, a discectomy on my lower spine and a left-thumb surgery to extricate a tree branch that was rooting for me (actually, through me). In the aftermath of both, a direct effect from prescribed painkillers, I became bound and determined - correction, I just became bound, really bound; after the spinal surgery, eight days bound. The pain from all my surgeries combined didn't hurt like this mounting pressure. When the moment of delivery came, I felt a whole new appreciation for moms in labor. So, I pled to the doctor to give me something to counteract what I knew *wouldn't* be coming. He wrote a prescription. He also asked the nurse to mix up for me a large glass of Mira LAX to-go - home, that is.

Mari had missed all this dialogue as she had stepped out of my room for a few minutes. Upon reentering the room and before anyone caught her out of the corner of their eye, and obviously thirsty, she downed the whole glass of what-she-presumed-was-water. *"Oh my!"* I had survived a quadruple bypass and a patient-gone-postal, only to die on the route home by a NASCAR Sprint Cup chauffeur. We flew home; and I'm clutching my heart pillow as tightly as I can, trying to absorb the shock of every bump en route. It was the railroad tracks aside the Nazareth Diner, however, that did me in. I saw the Gate of Heaven as my wife hit them at about 40 mph around a tight 90° turn! We traversed the 30-minute trip in under 20 - considerably under 20. Whirling into our driveway, Mari slammed on the breaks, threw open her door and tore into the house to ... Meantime, I sat in the car, in far too much pain to move, let alone exit. 45 minutes later – not really; just seemed that way to helpless me.

When Mari finally came out to retrieve and escort me inside, she situated me "comfortably" on our sofa. I remember reflecting over the past few days. Near-death by a major cardiac surgery. Near-death by a patient-gone-postal. Near-death by a Dale Earnhardt Jr. wannabe. Unless I was a cat in human-clothing with six more lives to go, I was about done with near-death brushes.

Now that I was back at home, I wasted no time in piggybacking on the dual-shoulders of my AD/HD and perfectionism to obey every dictate and nuance of my cardiac team. Within three weeks of my quadruple bypass, I would be back at work. Admittedly, a tad slow at first, but faithfully plodding along. I wasn't about to squander whatever time I might have left to complete whatever work God still had for me to do. In the ensuing days and weeks, the Divine message became manifestly clear: God wasn't finished with me yet.

Returning to fulltime ministry had proven beyond satisfying; it was all good - for a while. But all churchgoers know there is no such entity as a Perfect Church. Why? Because they attend. They get it that because a church comprises people like themselves, like me, who are flawed by nature and substantiate such regularly, the Perfect Church exists only as an oxymoron.

Whether due to my degenerative arterial condition or an ever-widening philosophical variance with my church, or likely both, and after many an emotionally-draining elder meeting and a plethora of intensive prayer sessions, I submitted my resignation just under two years post my surgery. Don't think I didn't wrestle with my failure syndrome, despite feeling squeezed between the proverbial *"rock and a hard place."* Did those former self-flagellations of "Failure" resurface during and afterwards? Count on it! Had I made mistakes along that four-year path that I would've done differently given a second chance? Probably. But if I had learned one thing from my past parade of failures is to confess them and move on in the embrace of God's tender Mercy. So rather than play the onerous game of second guessing, much less wallow in the self-pity of brooding-over, I knew God had more in store for me yet.

Every so often I reflect on that hard decision to resign. Oftentimes, I have been comforted from a simple reading of God's Word. One day I was reading the Old Testament account when the nation of Israel began its spiral decline with the splitting of the nation into two. King Rehoboam of Judah, motivated by greed and control and acting out of arrogance and inflexibility, mobilized his army to subjugate the northern 10 tribes of Israel. He'd show them you can't walk out on him. But just before brothers faced off against brothers and the Messianic line became exposed to potential obliteration, God stepped in with this command: *"Do not fight against your relatives. Go back home, for what has happened is My doing."* Rehoboam relented and both nations parted somewhat peaceful ways.

Christians concur uniformly that God desires unity among His people. But it appears that sometimes He allows division to occur to accomplish other - greater? - purposes we can't see at the time of the "break-up". Only later - and in ineffable ways! - as He would do in my circumstance.

My Head Was Out of It

While I was seeking God's direction for my uncertain future, several friends, but especially Glenn, asked me to consider starting a new church. My initial reaction - and one that protracted over several weeks - could best be captured in what I repeatedly said to myself during those uncertain days: *"What? Are you nuts?"* As much as I enjoy new adventures, I felt this one bordered insanity. I more than wrestled against the idea of going down this path; and for two credible reasons:

first, I wasn't the youthful dude fresh out of seminary with new and big dreams. I wasn't even the seasoned middle-aged pastor who better understood the demands of ministry and the sometimes-fickle nature of parishioners. I now stood at the threshold of my senior years with less energy and occasional "senior moments". I just didn't think I possessed the energy needed for this undertaking. I marvel at the biblical spy and war hero, Caleb, who led his troops into battle to conquer their piece of the Promised Land; not just because he distinguished himself with peerless faith, but by this time in the unfolding Israelite drama, he had advanced to the ripe old age of 85! I'd love to know what was in that manna that he had digested for those 40 years!

But second, as a direct result for having served for nearly four decades in ministry, experience had validated my prior biblical knowledge of man's nature. We can be frivolous in our commitments. We tend to hop aboard the latest and more enticing bandwagons. But when the initial enthusiasm wanes, the numbers start to dwindle, and the pastor is left holding the responsibility-bag - and a near-empty offering plate. What many shared at the outset, only a faithful few helped tote the bag - and "fill" the plate.

Enough interested people, however, convinced me to at least probe the possibility of beginning a new work. Glenn and his wife, Linda invited 27 friends to meet at their house on an otherwise mundane Saturday evening in March of 2013, the 23rd to be exact (OCD). Now one hour and 37 minutes (OCD) before this gathering, when my mind was leap-frogging all over the emotional map, I turned to Mari in our kitchen, grabbed her one hand, hoisting it with mine into the air, looked upwards towards Heaven and implored God inquiring, *"Father, You know I never ask for a sign; but I could sure use a little direction right about now."*

On this occasion, God wasted little time in answering me - and in the most dramatic fashion imaginable. Hollywood couldn't have scripted a better screen play.

God's Voice Was in It

The evening kicked off with a pot luck meal, which if this had been the extent to what the night held, it still would have been a more-than-satisfying evening; because among many other palate pleasers, Linda baked especially for me an extravagantly moist triple chocolate cake - with lavishly thick milk chocolate icing.

After 20 minutes of the usual socializing, exchange of greetings and catch-up on, *"What's been happening?"*, I stood encircled by my many friends. I shared for 20 minutes where *"I was at"* and what my thoughts were about *"Where do I go from here?"* I laid out three possible scenarios, the last of which was what some were hoping to hear, the establishment of a new church. I also shared quite honestly my fears for such considering the two reasons I stated above.

When I had finished sharing my prepared thoughts, I turned to everyone else and asked for their thoughts and feelings. Only a handful of folks unveiled their aspirations before 84-year old Ray Snyder, the E.F. Hutton among us *("When E.F. Hutton speaks, people listen.")*, calmly spoke for less than two minutes. He complimented others for how they had helped him in his spiritual growth and that he'd prefer to stay together to continue this maturation-trajectory. Knowing we would need a place to meet, he wisely added, *"We can worship Jesus anywhere. If He could be born in a barn, then we can certainly worship Him in one too."* Bringing his thoughts to a crescendo, though in his quiet and unassuming tone, Ray offered but a few more words of encouragement and hope. He possessed no idea that his words would be the very seeds that God would use to plant a new church. Deb P, as she is fondly called, did that night what she had done at every meeting she had ever attended in her life (guess she's got OCD too). She took verbatim notes and recorded Ray's last words: *"The Lord would like nothing more than for us to be united with Him and with each other."*

It wasn't any depth to Ray's words that stood out, but they resounded like a thunderclap when God echoed His *"Amen!"* For when Ray had finished speaking and I had offered my typical, *"Thanks Ray; really appreciate your thoughts,"* God shouted from Heaven. I had just turned around to face most everybody else with the words, *"Who'll be next?"* perched on my lips. I never did get the chance to utter them, for I had no sooner turned my back to Ray when I heard the other Debbie, who was sitting next to him, apprehensively inquire, *"Ray, Ray, you okay?"* I turned back around to see Ray fold his hands and slump listlessly in his chair as his eyes rolled back in his head. Immediately and eternally he was *"united with Him"*. Yes, these were Ray's *last* words, this side of eternity. Of course, we desperately tried to revive him until the EMTs arrived. Thank God it wasn't random that a few of the folks held CPR certification. Like a trained team, they diligently worked unabated with professionalism and focus, offering Ray his best chance of survival.

Once the ambulance team arrived, they went into high gear, hooking Ray up to all the necessary apparatus to try and revive him. Spontaneously, John's deep bass voice broke the tension, and immediately others joined him in chorus singing the strains to *"Amazing Grace."* Mari and I followed the ambulance to the nearest ER. But God had spoken; Ray was merely His Voice Box to all who would listen. Fulfilling the first part of God's message in "breath-taking" fashion - Ray's literally and everyone else's figuratively, he became *"united with Him"*. It now fell into the court of the rest of us to implement the second part and be *"united with each other"*. That is, would we start a new church?

If our church was conceived on March 23rd, then it was birthed on May 5th when we held our first worship service. During that interim and quite brief gestation period, we speedily strategized everything pertinent to getting started. From choosing a fitting name to drafting a church constitution and from targeting a ripe harvest field to seeking an appropriate facility, we hit the ministry-ground sprinting.

Hearing the story how we chose our name both peaks people's interest, while it unveils what sets us apart as unique. I recommended to our leadership team that we hold a contest, giving everyone who had decided to launch with us the opportunity to submit "write-in" name suggestions. I figured this way we would spur a modicum of interest, while reinforcing our commitment to be a church of the congregation, by the congregation and for the congregation. In other words, from the very outset, we wished to trumpet the message that everyone who attends our church will be valued and appreciated for who they are and whatever they have to offer.

We didn't limit the number of submissions anyone could make - because I was confident we would only receive perhaps a dozen - tops. One week and 57 name suggestions later, I faced my first church crisis. When people create something, anything, they become tenacious in arguing its surpassing value to anything else of its kind. The creation of a church name proved no different. I got that. I soon realized how passionate each person became over his or her name choice. I confess, I campaigned for mine; if for no other reason, it was the best! I just needed to convince everybody else it was the best.

We knew we needed to whittle down the number of possibilities; especially since no church sign could accommodate these many names. So, we held our first democratic vote. The leadership team thought we should take the top 10 and then hold a second election to narrow the choices down to three. Now I must have campaigned well, because the name I created - the best of the lot by far - made it to the final run-off election. How could we not somehow honor the man whose extraordinarily-timed death gave us life? I submitted, *"Ray of Hope Church."*

I ordered a recount when the best name by far came in second. No, I didn't. I merely sulked for a week. No, I didn't do that either; just two days. But I did realize almost immediately how fitting was the name that took top honors, *"Faith Family Fellowship."* We are an assembly of folks who fervently believe that a vital and growing relationship with God is built on a profound **faith** in the historic teachings of the Bible. We are a **family** that enjoys a closeness that transcends even the kinship of the biologic family. We are a **fellowship**, sharing from who we are, with what we have.

Faith Family Fellowship was up and running. Well almost. The law had more to say in this regard – a lot more – pages and pages of legalese more, to obtain the coveted 501c3 non-profit status. I contacted Rich Hopkins, one of my friends from my first pastorate. Rich is a lawyer and knew everything we needed to do. So, he not only streamlined our application process, he piloted us through every step – all 737 of them. Some would argue that what Rich did for us counts as our second big miracle. Why? Because Rich provided all his service at NO cost. A free lawyer! Yeah, this may just count as a miracle.

Now we were up and running.

God's Hand Was in It

Launching a new church presents many challenges: money, a core of spiritual leaders, a critical mass of committed volunteers, gaining and sustaining momentum, money, knowing what priorities to take on first, communicating the vision and enticing buy-in - and money. But of these impediments, which presents the highest hurdle to overcome? Not what you may think despite my tease; it's not the almighty dollar when you trust the Almighty Donor. From the outset, even when the fervor of newness resembled a young couple welcoming their firstborn into the world, I echoed a resounding message: *"We need our own building."* Though our "doors had been open" for only a couple of months, we didn't actually have doors to open. And without a facility to call our own, whether owned or rented, we possessed no vivacity or visibility, and thus no viability in the community. We lived week by week at the mercy of two other establishments providing us sufficient space to conduct our worship services.

The primary place that opened its doors to us was a sister church in the area, Maranatha Family Christian Fellowship. The members there allowed us to use their sanctuary on alternating Saturday evenings and Sunday afternoons; and this they granted at no cost! What a gracious provision to a new work that needed every dollar to launch and sail.

The other place that opened its doors to us proved mutually beneficial. We gained a meeting place while a local personal care home enjoyed a worship service. Once per month, we combined our entire church family of 40 folks with the wonderful seasoned citizens of Alexandria Manor. I'm still uncertain as to who received the greater blessing!

Faith Family Fellowship will be forever indebted to these two local organizations. Regarding the latter, we still hold a monthly worship service there for the sake of the dear residents. But our church knew we needed our own place, if we wanted to celebrate beyond our first and second birthdays. So almost from the start of our ministry, from the summer of 2013, we began to pray for a miracle. Why a miracle? Because our church family was small, and we had zero funds towards a purchase. But not only so, we squeezed God into two very tight provisional corners. The first corner had to do with debt. When we had organized, we vowed not to go into debt. Now by committing ourselves to this ideal, we didn't mean we would never take on a mortgage. What we did mean was that we would only assume a mortgage that would translate into a minimum of 25% down with our monthly principal not to exceed the cost of a small rental. But our leadership team believed that Almighty God could demonstrate His Almightiness once again. And second, we told God where He should provide us a facility. (Ever notice how we typically call the spiritual shots and then ask God to bless our desires: *"Not Your will, but ours be done?"*) Well, we weren't exactly guilty in this regard. We had prayed for wisdom and believed the Holy Spirit was leading us to open a church in a locale where we wouldn't be treading on another evangelical church's turf. We pinpointed a "major" intersection on our map of Upper Nazareth (one of the few 4-way stop sign intersections) and drew an imaginary 3 in. diameter circle around it. Somewhere in this zone, God would play Realtor and Buyer and get us a home.

Summer slipped into fall and we were still homeless. But on another of those *Random Cosmic Occurrences*, a couple from our church drove past an old church building that was hosting an Antique Sale that very day. Not many of our families would've been baited by the advertising sign out on the lawn, but Steve and Gail collect antiques. Steve made an unplanned turn into the parking lot and within moments, they were strolling through the edifice and even made a purchase. But upon exiting the building, Gail's eyes happened (*Random Cosmic Occurrence?)* to light on this inconspicuous 3 x 5 index card off to the side that most people certainly missed. It looked more like a post-it reminder for the owner than an advertisement for the public. But the three words scribbled on this card stopped Gail in her tracks. She had to inquire about the meaning behind: *"Building for Sale."* Granted, it too was an antique, the cornerstone betraying its age. Erected in 1873. But was it for sale as well? Turning to the nearest person, she asked, *"Do you know anything about this notice?"*

The person declined any knowledge but pointing to a man standing nearby, she did say, *"That's the owner right there."*

Gail, already envisioning the answer to our prayer with the pews filled with our folks, boldly approached this unsuspecting figure. She asked, *"I'm wondering about the little note by the exit, 'Building for Sale.'"*

Because Gail was so caught up in her fanciful projections of the *"what could be,"* she couldn't recall much else than this. The owner explained quite matter-of-factly, *"My wife and I are retiring to North Carolina next month. We're selling our house."* Allow me to dispel the fog: The church building had been converted to a residence about 20 years earlier when Ed & Joy Face had purchased it. But for the prior 120 years, *Jehovah Church*, existed for the purpose it was originally constructed, to serve the community with the light of the Gospel of Jesus Christ. The Face's initially bought the property to open an Antique business, but circumstances compelled them to open an addiction-recovery ministry there instead. They refurbished the below-ground floor into a residence and preserved the sanctuary for this ministry.

Now before I proceed further with this unfolding story, I must interject something very telling about this couple. They personify humility. Let me explain by borrowing from the trademark lines of the popular TV show that spanned the decade in which I was born, Dragnet. In a droning monotone, the narrator opened each episode with these memorable words, *"Ladies and Gentlemen, the story you are about to hear is true. Only the names have been changed to protect the innocent."* Similarly, the story you are about to hear is true, only the names have been changed to honor their request. They asked I withhold their real names because they didn't want to draw any attention to what they might do; they wanted all approbation to be given to God. Thus, I chose the names Joy Face because her face radiates Joy, and Eddie, because his role in this drama reminds us that the true Church is never about an *edifice*, it's about people; it's not about *Eddie Face*; it's about a humble man and woman who put God first in their lives. So, we pick up where we left off.

Gail continued the dialogue by saying, *"Our new church is looking for a facility. Is there any possibility you would have interest in selling your house to a church?"*

The brief encounter concluded with Eddie suggesting, *"Why don't you bring some of your leaders over one night this week and we can discuss the possibility?"*

I'm sure Gail hadn't made it back to her car before she had phoned my cell and rambled on about our *"just perfect"* new home. Her excitement spilled over and became mine almost instantaneously. She shared Eddie's invitation and gave me his phone number. Because Gail told me the antique sale would last till 5pm that evening, I impatiently waited till 5:01 to call. No, that's not true. But what was true was my eager anticipation to follow-up, and the heart-to-heart conversation I had with God over the course of the next several hours. If my memory serves me well, I had waited till the next morning to call the Face's. Like I scripted earlier, it's at times like these that the line between Divine Sovereignty and human responsibility blurs. How much do I trust God that this situation was safely cupped in His Hands and at what point do I pick up the phone? I presumed, however, that I must act soon. I certainly didn't want to be the one responsible for letting this golden-platter opportunity slip through God's Hands. Oh me, of little faith.

Meantime, my mind started to play those disheartening mental *"What if?"* games: *"What if another and wealthier church comes along and outbids us?"* *"What if the Face's set the price too high for our commitment to avoid debt?"* *"What if the building burns down right after we come to terms?"* *"What if? What if? What if?"*

"Really Bob, where's your trust? Are you really going to permit your bent to negativity outmuscle your faith in God?" I recognized the Holy Spirit's *"Voice"* bringing me back to point. *"Do you really think Random Cosmic Occurrences control the ebb and flow of life? Haven't*

I declared that 'I make known the end from the beginning, from ancient times, what is still to come'? And haven't I repeatedly proven that 'My purpose will stand, and I will do all that I please. What I have said, that I will bring about; what I have planned, that I will do?'" (see Bible: Isaiah 46:10-11 NIV)

"Lord, You know I'm a slow learner. You know I identify with that dejected dad of the demon-possessed son who cried out, 'I believe! But help me overcome my unbelief." (see Bible: Mark 9:24)

After sharing this beyond-wonderful news with the church family the next morning at worship, most of us were convinced we had a permanent home-of-our-own with the Jehovah Church on Bushkill Center Rd. in Upper Nazareth. I couldn't sit still for the next couple of days until we had this sure-thing conversation with the Face's. I remember walking up to their door, ringing the bell, hearing their dog bark and being escorted into their living room. As our leadership team approached Joy, she made a conspicuous, though unintentional gesture. She suddenly bent forward and grabbed her stomach. I remember grabbing her hand and quietly asking her, *"Are you okay?"* Never having met the woman, I didn't know if she had been battling an intestinal bug that day or if she was prone to seizures. I just remember how awkward a moment it was; but she said nothing – at the time.

We exchanged introductions, after which Joy and her husband, Eddy, led us on a tour of their house. Not one opinion varied from the conviction that their home was tailor-made for us - just one more confirmation that Faith Family Fellowship had a new home. The path to this purchase appeared clutter-free and it was just a matter of time before this building, after a 20-year hiatus, would be reestablished as a church. For me, the deal was signed and sealed just a few days later, during a subsequent conversation with Joy. I never expected to hear what I did when we were discussing the *"What's the next step?"* in our negotiations. Joy refreshed my memory of the night we met and that awkward moment of her belly flop. She then spoke words that immediately seared into my conscience, *"The moment I laid eyes on your people coming towards me, I knew our house would be your home – for the Holy Spirit leapt within me."* She believed this physical anomaly was God's sign that her house would soon be our church home. Now because of my parade of recent RCO's, I didn't discard her strange words as readily as I once would have done. In fact, and certainly because of my desperation for wanting a church home, I clung to her words as tightly as I grip my commitment to the Bible.

In reviewing the minutes of our Leadership Team meeting of October 18th, we recorded Deb P's words of faith: *"It seems like the Holy Spirit is already there waiting for us."* And if you hadn't already guessed, yes, the building even sat in the epicenter of the geographical area we "knew" God wanted us to settle! All we needed to do now was await God's miracle to raise the 25% down-payment based on the agreed sale price of $260K - or $65K.

Just to ensure that the transference of title would be a done-deal, I jumped on the suggestion of one of my pastor friends at one of our monthly fellowship gatherings. Five of us attended on this day that Pastor Sean recommended we *"head over to the church now, lay our hands on the four corners of the building and individually pray for God's Will to be done."* (I think I interjected what that Will must be. Nothing like letting God be God.) So, Pastors Jim, Ken, Matt, Sean and I put a hold on our meeting to take care of the greater business. It's a good thing this building only had four corners or some of the building would have gone un-blessed. (Kidding.) So, my four brothers each knelt before one of the four corners while I knelt before the front doors. Each at our station, we asked God to please open these doors for our church family - and in turn, the greater community.

Now keep in mind, our church had only been in operation for a mere six months. But in this brief lapse of time, some of our members began to lapse. Meeting on Saturday evenings and Sunday afternoons was not our preferred option, but at the time, it was our only option due to space availability. The church that had been sharing its facility with us could not have been more accommodating and generous over this sustained period. It never feared competition, as seems to be an uncomplimentary blemish on too many churches today. But even given this blessing, some of our church families' commitment had slowly leaked like an aging tire. So, the miracle God needed to perform would have to be even greater than the miracle He could have performed but a few months back when we enjoyed more financial backing.

We never lost sight of our resolute vow to not enter debt. So, in November 2013, we initiated our first (and only, thus far) fundraising campaign. With our 20 families, we believed God's miracle translated into raising the $65,000 - within three months! Now trust me when I say we did not have those two or three families who were independently wealthy and could double others' individual pledges. In fact, we didn't have even one! But as for those on the other end of the financial spectrum, we were amply blessed.

We ran a very simple campaign, entitled *"Fleecing the Flock"* - just kidding - that asked for no monies up front. Stating our targeted sum of $65K, we merely requested that all pledges be made by January 31st of 2014. If we didn't see God's miracle provision by that date, we would interpret this whole process as God's test of our resolve to stay clear of debt. To demonstrate how sincere we were about this commitment, I share here an excerpt from the letter we sent out to our church folks and other friends dated November 4, 2013:

"... we at FFF desire to be fiscally responsible and are both ***praying and trusting first*** *for God's clear indication and then for* ***His miracle****. Without BOTH, we will not proceed ... Now if it is God's Spirit Who has spoken, then this purchase will be nothing short of a miracle. And why? Because we have zero funds towards a purchase. But if God*

could do the greater by parting the Red Sea so His chosen people of old could enter their Promised Land, then He can certainly do the lesser and purchase the Red-brick church so his chosen people of FFF can enter their Proposed Land.

So why am I writing to you? We believe this facility has been handed to us a on a silver platter with many clear God-signs. We just don't have the silver for the platter. This is where our name Faith is being challenged. But please understand, we do not wish to race ahead of Him, but equally, we do not wish to lag behind Him. We simply want to honor Him in every way we possibly can. Having our own facility would provide us more stability, visibility and productivity within the greater community. Therefore, would you pray with us for God's clear Will for us? Beyond this, if and only if you feel so inclined to help with a onetime financial gift, we would ask that all you do at this time is to let Glenn R. know... We will then total all verbal pledges and interpret the response as God's signal one way or the other, whether we should proceed or let go for now. Let me be clear: I am asking that you NOT send the gift at present in the event that God shows us we are NOT to proceed with the purchase. In that event, please use your monetary blessing to bless some other ministry or charity of your own choosing. We will be most content with obedience, not a building. We are the Church God is building. The building is simply a facility to facilitate ministry."

No big deal for God to raise the needed $65K. But was this our faith speaking, or was this our human hubris proudly grinning? I had deemed God's miracle would come in the form of our small congregation raising the very large down-payment monies necessary to qualify for a mortgage. I was so confident that God would supply the need that I telephoned the Face's, now enjoying the bliss of retirement in North Carolina, to ask if we could hold a Christmas Eve service in what was still their property, just not their home. I was so sure it would soon be our home. They excitedly gave us permission and we eagerly turned back the sanctuary clock by transforming the holy hall to its former use. A handful of women beautified the room with greens, bows and candles. What they did to that room could have been photographed and embossed on Christmas cards by Hallmark. The serenity and simple beauty took our breath away.

We had to let the greater community know about this remarkable event, so I scripted this invitation, which I have copied here in full. We printed the "Tale" on the obverse of the invitation and "Our Hope" on the reverse.

A Tale of Two Trees

This tree, stately and full, only looks to be live, but is indeed dead. Don't be fooled by its vibrant forest green color. Having been severed from its root base, the source of its vitality, it casts but the illusion of life. Its deceptive appearance is merely marking time before every needle falls to betray its true estate.

This tree, barren and ominous, looks to be dead, but is indeed live. For on this tree hung the Indestructible God-man, Who bridged the impassable chasm that divided Holy God from sinful man. He too was severed from His root base, from His Heavenly Father, but only while fulfilling the mission of this tree.

We are the fir, with all the appearance of life. But unless we have individually looked to that barren tree, our needles will continue to fall until there are none. Please consider "decorating" your home this year with this Live Tree, so you can experience Real Life.

Our Christmas Hope for You

I'm sure you have never read *"A Tale of the Two Trees"* before because we authored it just for this Christmas season. But it is quite likely you have heard countless times before the timeless tale it conveys. It is nothing other than the story that marks its beginning at that first and history-altering Christmas. It's the story where the Creator of the Universe chose to garb Himself within the flesh of His crowning creative achievement, you and me. Christmas is all about how God stooped down to become one of us, so we could become united with Him, and forever enjoy the **REAL LIFE** He offers. We, the church of Faith Family Fellowship would love nothing more than to share with you this greatest of all Christmas gifts, **Jesus' gift of eternal life**.

This being said, we wish to **invite you** ... to attend the

Reopening of the Jehovah Union Church on Christmas Eve for a Candlelight Service at 7pm

What a night! The sanctuary that had only held memories of the Holy Spirit of Christmases Past came to life by the same Holy Spirit of the Christmas Present. Soft candles flickering on the sills before the 140-year old stained-glass windows, coupled with the ancient carols and Gospel readings, made this evening even more a *silent night, holy night*. If ever a church facility was tailor-made for our church family, this had to be the one. Everybody sensed this, many even voicing this. Yet we wanted to keep our emotions in check, so our desire didn't outdistance our faith.

At one point during the service, I opened the floor so that everyone had an opportunity to share *"the one gift you would love to discover under your Christmas tree this year."* I don't believe anyone got that opportunity before Big Ed's voice bellowed from the back pew, *"The deed!"* An eruption of *"Amens!"* confirmed that as a church, we desired nothing more than for God to have a House where He could meet with us routinely.

When we stepped outside the building following the service, quarter-sized snowflakes were cascading from the darkened skies and a coverlet of snow had already put the final touches on our Thomas Kinkaid "painting". Rides home proved precarious, but thankfully, no incidents occurred. But we didn't learn till we gathered for our next Saturday evening worship service that the snow had fallen only on a three-mile radius surrounding the Jehovah Church. How could we not interpret this as God smiling down on us and blanketing us 'neath His cloak of confirmation? This was going to be our home!

Our campaign proved successful! - just NOT in the way we had envisioned. We already "saw" the deed in hand, the front doors wide open on Sundays (No more Saturday evenings!) and the neighborhood folks filling our pews. Instead, what God provided was His Smile. Despite the excitement that ensued from this hodgepodge of 20 income-earning families that had pledged some $40,000, we still fell woefully short of our cut-off point. $40K was an incredible miracle in and of itself, and pushed us to the precipice of temptation to negotiate on our resolve. But we had prayed and vowed to *"Just say No!"* to anything less than $65K. There are few emotions in life more satisfying than knowing you just passed a God-test. But I confess, I wonder if my (our) resolve would've held firm if we pledged say, $62K? *"Thank You, Lord, that You do 'not tempt us above what we are able to resist.'"* (see Bible: 1 Corinthians 10:13)

Keeping our success in perspective proved hard; for we were elated we pleased God, but were disheartened that He didn't please us - at least not in the way we had anticipated. All those clear indications, those God-sightings that cannot be explained away as but *Cosmic Random Occurrences*; especially Joy Face's ethereal visit from the Holy Spirit Who had confirmed in her twisting tummy the sale being as good as done. Evidently, she had misinterpreted the effects of an evening side of undigested jalapeno peppers. It was as though God had rained on our celebration parade. But being the pastor, I had to sustain a good front. Sure, I identified with everyone else's sadness. Add to this my negative bent and failure-complex. Nevertheless, I had to offer some credible explanation to our congregation. Yes, I was conflicted; and I knew that whatever I voiced, would be somewhat disingenuous, though still heartfelt. I tried to rally everyone behind my banner cry that *"Since God closed on us this door, it only means He has something better in store."*

I knew what I was saying was indeed true, and could therefore say what I said. But I also knew my heart was lagging far behind my head. Always being a baseball buff, I couldn't help but interpret the closing door on Jehovah Church as *"Strike one!"* Then to make the matter even more emotionally unsettling, two of our once-committed families chose to leave our church at that time. My negative-bent and failure-complex couldn't restrain from unloading more self-critical deprecation.

That winter seemed especially cold, colder than any I remembered; and not just because it broke several low temperature records. Was it the extreme weather that contributed to the greater number of empty pews on Saturday nights, or were more families growing cold in their hearts to the dream once shared?

The spring of 2014 didn't arrive fast enough. Even then, my heart took longer to thaw. But just when it was scraping the bottom of its emotional barrel, another *Random Cosmic Occurrence* brought us to the front door of another facility. Was God unveiling His *"something better"* in the form of a sister church that enjoyed the exclusive use of a facility, but no pastor, while our church had just the opposite? Our congregation remembers salivating over the facility when we first toured it, newly refurbished with everything needed for the kind of services we offered. Now admittedly, we felt a tad confused why it wasn't in the location we believed God had called us to minister. But He knows where the needs are, and where our church could best accommodate those needs. So, we weren't about to correct God's reshuffling. Nonetheless, we were excited about the prospect of combining two churches into one as a demonstration of God's unifying work.

Following my baseball analogy, God's voice pierced our already wounded hearts, *"Strike two!"* He closed this door of opportunity on us almost as quickly as it had opened. Did this other church wish to sustain its autonomy? Did it wonder if some of its higher goals might get lost in the shuffle of reorganization? Did it deem it could hire a better pastor than the one on the table? I preferred to think it was either or both of the first two possibilities. Nonetheless, I know I was supposed to continue proclaiming to my church family, while desperately clinging to the vestiges of my failing faith, that the *"something better"* meant there was *"something better"* yet!

When I mused long enough over my own somewhat-insincere words, my imaginations would keep flashing these mental pictures of what an awesome place God must be preparing for our church. With all these delectable carrots He'd been dangling before our carnal faces, WOW! what would His final unveiling reveal?? Meanwhile, my negative bent perseverated over the thought, *"When God's miracle revelation finally provided us a building, would there be any church members left to sit in its pews?"*

I also wrestled over the whole *"faith without works is dead"* principle. I kept jostling between how much I should do to demonstrate my faith, all along that spectrum from nothing-but-prayer to something-only-the-Holy-Spirit. I recall one day at the end of April, being persuaded by an inner voice - was it God's or mine? I still can't say. Nevertheless, I phoned the Face's with purposeful intent. We exchanged sincere pleasantries, for in the few brief winter months of negotiation we got to know each other, a genuine friendship blossomed. Then I got down to the business of my call. *"Eddie, I still see your 'For Sale' sign on the front lawn of your house. No luck yet, huh? I was wondering, if perchance, we could rent from you, until the house sells. Might you even consider a lease-to-purchase provision?"*

Very sympathetically, Eddie explained what made real sense: *"We don't feel we should place ourselves at risk. Would you be able keep the place clean for the realtor to show the place at a moment's notice? Or worse, how 'bout if somebody gets injured on the premises? Where we do we draw the line of responsibility?"* He made perfect sense, so I thanked him for hearing me out and offered him God's best on the future sale. So, it was clear that the church doors God had closed back in January when our fundraising campaign fell short, He now locked in April when our offer to rent was denied.

Did you ever notice how slowly life drags on when you're fearing the apparent inevitable? Summer was looming near, and our numbers continued to dwindle. The elders began to broach the one subject we fought hard to resist; but maybe God was closing all the doors because they were meant to be closed. Our attendance was trickling down to a couple of handfuls - on a good Saturday evening. We hadn't voted on this yet, but we discussed how and when to wrap up shop.

I would have been a fool not to guard my heart when we learned about the *"Red Barn"* God flashed before us next. This one-time restaurant had just finished being remodeled for additional public purposes, and just happened to be owned by Steve and Gail's (remember them?) relatives. Now granted, any contractual agreement would be but a temporal fix as this was a rental property. But except for this less-than-best scenario, in other ways it proved even better than the Jehovah Church. Even more Divine signals lit up the pathway to its usage, like the realization this facility was literally a *"barn"*, just like our E.F. Hutton had ordered. But on the day before we were to sign a contract, this door suddenly slammed shut! *"Strike three, you're out!"*

But this isn't baseball, so what did this mean for FFF? We were clearly *"out"* of a building. Every door that had started to open, closed. We were despairingly *"out"* of emotional gas. Like a sputtering auto on a barren strip of desert highway with no filling stations in sight, we felt hopeless. We were realistically *"out"* of time. The clock of survivability was nearing the midnight hour, and we all knew it. This almost-visible dark cloud of despondency hovered thick over our entire church family, all 25 men, women and children that had remained. God had rained down on our parade one final time. I felt atop my head to ensure my pastoral hat hadn't blown off. It hadn't; so, I mustered up sufficient energy to spout off what was as much a self-exhortation as a congregational appeal: *"Don't lose faith, folks. God has something better!"*

The summer solstice failed to warm up my ever-chilling heart; and the same could be said of so many of the so few left. Our enthusiasm kept dissipating like the air in a 10-day old helium balloon. We had to place our hope for a miracle on life support. The minutes from our June 5th elders meeting reflected our desperation: *"FFF Needs to transition to Sunday morning worship services if we're to survive as a congregation."* Nagging echoes of *"Failure"* ping-ponged back and forth between my head and my heart. It would take another miracle now just to hoist me back on board the ship of hope.

Christy, one of the few remaining Faithful's, called me one mid-June day to tell me about a nature preserve and conference center located near her home. She had done some preliminary investigative work and felt it would at least keep our life support switch turned on. But for more than a few reasons, this alternative didn't qualify as a miracle in my lexicon. It was so secluded, even the neighbors didn't know it was there. It lay 5 miles outside our target zone. And it was not the most inviting place to entice visitors - at least not those of the two-legged variety. If this was God's miracle-in-the-making, I wanted a do-over, or a reeducation as to His definition of "miracle". Besides, we already had our three strikes, and we all know what this means: we were *"Out!"*

The Jehovah Church was strike one. The two-into-one blended church was strike two. The *"red barn"* was strike three. So, when this opportunity arose, I had already rewritten the game of baseball when I shouted out in the recesses of my own heart, *"Strike four!"* Nevertheless, I'd play along until the Divine Umpire bellowed, *"You're out!"* I guess I was still clinging onto the thread of hope for God's miracle; so, I placed a call to this establishment. The owner greeted me very kindly and cooperatively, and I could tell he seemed genuinely accommodating. He helped me clutch tighter to the rope of my hope. However, if this rope snapped, then I knew God was pulling the plug to our life support. I was already mentally scripting the eulogy I would give for our one-year and one-month old church.

Instead of scripting our epitaph, however, I drafted a call-to-recommitment letter. If our ship was destined to sink, I at least wanted to feel I had sent out one final SOS to the church family. None of our members required a keen sense for reading between the lines to realize this was my penultimate letter as pastor of Faith Family Fellowship. Listen to the real message behind these excerpted words:

"We're all familiar with the expression, 'caught between a rock and a hard place.' If you pause to look closely, you will see me sandwiched right there. The 'rock' is the reality of where we are as a church and the 'hard place' is my ministry-long practice to not 'meddle' in my people's minds, especially since the perception may appear to be self-serving... I pondered and prayed long and hard over this and concluded that spiritual leadership means taking risks that could be misconstrued, and/or my motives misread...

*When God gave birth to **Faith Family Fellowship** just over a year ago, there was the expected enthusiasm. The 'cheers' could be heard as we bolted out of the starting gate. But because this is a marathon and not a mile race, our spiritual adrenaline has since depleted and now we're sucking in air to endure the race. So, here's the challenge:*

*Do we still believe God has a **UNIQUE PLAN** for Faith Family Fellowship? Do we still believe that for any church to thrive we must **ALL** run the marathon race? And do we individually believe that **'I'** (meaning you/me) **MUST DO ALL I CAN** as part of my ultimate fulfillment to 'seek first the Kingdom of God'? On a personal note of commitment, I can't see myself doing anything other. Ray Snyder's prophetic words continue to spur me to greater service: **'God would like nothing more than for us to be united with Him and each other.'***

*Therefore, what am I asking from each of you this day? I'm asking you to **reevaluate where you are in your commitment both to Jesus and His local church called FFF**. We're at a crossroads. The statistics do not lean in our favor as 25% of new churches do not survive their* *first year, and the 75% that do, 'remain small with limited impact' (David T. Olson, Director of the American Church Research Project). BUT I refuse to let mere statistics be my spiritual guide. When Jesus bounded from the tomb, He knocked the stuffing out of all statistics. **WE CAN DO THIS! But it will take ALL OF US!**...*

*Thank you for taking the time to read this letter and hearing my plea. I would further ask you to pray that we soon land a rental location we can call our own. We need this visibility and stability, so we can congregate during that time most conducive for church growth - Sunday morning. We all too easily attest that **'God is able'**. But He has chosen to usually **exercise His Ability through the ministry of the local church**. This means each one of us must mount the altar of self-sacrifice daily!"*

The real message? The iceberg lay dead ahead and we're about to hit it. Unless God grabs the helm and diverts our ship, we're going down. This letter was dated June 27th, though I didn't email it until the following morning, just in time for God to grab the wheel and do what He does best: gives "do-over's" that showcase His impeccable timing and peerless Personality. FFF's 2nd jaw-dropping miracle was not only in-the-making, it was about to be revealed.

On this very morning, June 28th, while I was focused on our life-support meeting, God was orchestrating our resuscitate one. Earlier in the week, the owner of the nature-preserve and I had arranged to meet on the coming Saturday morning - June 28th. I remember getting up that day with precious little motivation as I had been interpreting God's writing on my heart's wall. Its echo-chambers kept reverberating, *"Do not resuscitate."* We agreed to meet on site at 11am. Now was it because I knew batters don't get four strikes, or had I eaten some bad eggs for breakfast? I don't know. What I do know is that my digestive track was competing in the men's all-around in gymnastics. My gut was a mess! Consequently, I couldn't dislodge myself from the bathroom that morning. The plan included picking up Christy on my way over to the interview. I had arranged with her, *"... about 10:45."* But at 10:35, I was still trying to pry myself from the potty. It was a 15-minute ride over to her house and another 5 to arrive on time. Well that wasn't going to happen. It needs to be clearly understood that I'm rarely ill and never run late - to anything (integrally riveted to my OCD and perfectionist leaning), but most especially something of this import.

Meanwhile, in the corridors that connect Heaven to earth, a message had been sent and received by a family in North Carolina. So, at 10:39am, on that destined-to-pull-the-plug Saturday, in response to having answered God's telephone call sometime during the night, this family telephoned ours. I ignored it because I was already running late. I guess an intestinal bug can serve as a *Random Cosmic Occurrence*?? Mari, however, picked up the phone and yelled through the bathroom door, who was on the other end, but added, *"They really want to speak with both of us. I told them you're already late for a meeting, but they asked for just one minute of your time."*

I _un_graciously picked up another receiver, while my mind was racing ahead to where I needed to be and rehearsing my apology for my tardiness. I quickly chirped in the perfunctory, *"Hey, how are you? Nice to hear from you,"* and then rudely reiterated what Mari had already stated - that I was running late for a meeting. I did offer to call back later in the day, so our conversation wouldn't be rushed.

But Eddie interrupted saying, *"This won't take but a moment."* Then together he and Joy said this: *"We wish to drop something in your church offering plate."*

I didn't quite know what to make of this, knowing who my callers were; my mind conjuring up all sorts of gifts, from a projector to a generous check. I said something to the effect, *"Oh, you obviously sold your house. Congratulations!"* Pretty logical deduction on my part, and quite a magnanimous gesture on theirs, to donate something to our church from the proceeds of their sale. I don't know if they even heard what I had just said, but it soon became apparent that I had drawn the wrong conclusion. They informed me, *"No, we haven't sold our house."* Yet they still wanted to drop something into our plate?

You've already connected enough of the disjointed dots to realize it was Joy and Eddie Face on the other end of the line. Theirs was the property that was our *"Strike one!"* in the search for a permanent church home. One of those pregnant pauses hung suspended in the air while everyone was waiting for the other person to speak, all four voices remaining conspicuously quiet for an uncomfortable moment. Finally, Joy broke the silence and probed, *"Well, don't you want to know what we wish to drop in your plate?"*

I don't recall my exact response, but I remember it was profoundly inane; something like, *"Sure."* Now it's instructive at this moment that you understand I am hard of hearing - and virtually deaf over a phone. So, when Eddie came back with his reply to the looming question, I pulled the phone away from my ear, shook it and faintly muttered, *"Operator, I must have a loose connection."*

Another pregnant pause - because I didn't know if my hearing deficit misheard what I had thought he had said, or whether there really was a loose connection. Then in almost rehearsed stereophonic harmony, together they exclaimed, *"The Deed."* Big Ed, and everyone else at Faith Family Fellowship, had just been given the best gift under our collective Christmas tree imaginable. The building of our pipedreams, suddenly became our reality.

People who know me well would testify that I'm rarely left speechless. This was one of those aberrant occasions. I stumbled for the right words, but I think my silence spoke louder than my feeble words. I remember one thing I asked that bordered coherence: *"What caused you to do an about Face? What caused you to change your mind?"* Originally, the Face's had offered us their home at 30K off the asking price. Why? Because they were delighted by the prospect that their home would once again serve the community as originally intended. It had served them as a comfortable home for 20 years, but now they were retired in North Carolina. Nothing gave them greater pleasure than to see this old building become a new church - again.

So, what caused Eddie and Joy to change their minds and gift their home to us instead of selling it? The Lord certainly knew they had the practical need to live off the proceeds of the sale to sustain them through their twilight years. They expounded upon their decision with something undeniably Sovereign. This was no *Random Cosmic Occurrence,* even for the quintessential skeptic. God had separately directed them during the early morning hours of the prior night to take their property off the market and offer it to us at a drastically-reduced asking price. Well how did He do that? I'll never forget their words, *"We both woke up this morning and turned to each other and said, 'I need to tell you something.'"* They both then disclosed their separate prior night's revelation, which was a revelation of the *Divine dream* variety - and it was the *same dream*! They wasted no time in placing the call that rekindled my hope and bolstered my faith. They agreed with God's asking price, perfectly matching the price Jesus asks in gifting to us His offer of eternal life: ABSOLUTELY FREE! (I confessed earlier that I'm not much of a God-speaks-to-us through dreams kind of guy; but I confess, I'm gravitating in a more open-minded direction.)

If this wasn't miracle enough, Joy placed the exclamation point on it. As we talked - which turned out to be more than *"just a minute of your time"*, though I kept it short to honor my prior commitment - she asked, *"Do you remember that first night and I had said to you"* -

She didn't get to finish her statement as I cut her off in mid-sentence and said, *"How could I ever forget your words?! They seared into my conscience that very night. Don't think they haven't reverberated in my mind at several critical moments ever since."* Then as though in stereophonic sound over the phone lines, we recited her unforgettable words in concert: *"I knew the moment I laid eyes on your people coming into our house, this would be your home - for the Holy Spirit leapt inside of me."* Silently, I smirked at the private memory for having repeatedly resisted a taunting temptation. Over the prior five months, I had yearned to "remind" Joy of her "confirmation" as the deed kept slipping further and further through our fingers. Joy went on to testify that she never diverted from that conviction. She didn't know when or how it would all come about, but she never drifted in her absolute persuasion that their home, which was really God's Home, would eventually become our home. She and Eddie had said to me early on during our negotiations, *"Our hope is to see our house become a church once again."* And so, it is: what had been their hope, has become our miracle; but both have always been nothing less than God's Perfect and Perfectly-Timed Plan. *Random Cosmic Occurrence??? Don't think so!!! Know so!!!*

"God did something better!" He took my bold-sounding words, though laced with undeniable traces of wavering faith, and outdid Himself. Three strikes and we were SAFE! Nothing short of a miracle! Yes, undeniably, Ray Snyder died and gave us life. Joy and Eddie Face died to self and resuscitated us back to life. But it was really God orchestrating His Will, His Way, in His time. In the end, He gave us so much more than the miracles of raising 65K, or gathering us in an E.F. Hutton *"barn"*, or meeting with us in the quietude of a secluded Garden of Eden. He handed us the golden platter of the ready-made Home we so wanted to call our own in the heart of the area we first believed God would place us. But more than this, He has opened to us a *real* set of church doors, so we can invite others in! His rain-on-our-parade is over, but His Reign-over-all is over-the-top!

Chapter 5
The Miracle That Keeps on Giving

If I hadn't made this point manifestly clear throughout, let me state it unequivocally here: There is nothing innately special about Faith Family Fellowship, nor did we do anything exceedingly spiritual that somehow merited an over-the-top favor by God. Every Divine Love tap upon our church shoulder issued from the Heart of the God Who overflows with Grace and Mercy. He delighted to do what He did on our behalf because this is Who He is. He is the Father Who takes Infinite Pleasure in caring for His children, and sometimes in miracles that carry us to the realm of the inconceivable.

Once we took official ownership of our miracle, we wanted to give it an interior face lift. Though it was in move-in condition, and even had the water, heat, A/C and electric all upgraded, we still wanted to give it a fresh coat of paint. The words, *"Simple, but beautiful"*, became our decorative shibboleth. (see Bible: Judges 12:1-6) Whatever we agreed to do, it would combine simplicity and beauty.

One afternoon Mari offered to go price paint. So, she hopped into her car and headed off to the local Home Depot - almost. A *Random Cosmic* road construction backed up traffic. This delay triggered Mari's impatience. So, she diverted her travel destination to drive the couple extra miles to the sister Home Depot in the next town. Upon arrival, she immediately headed for the paint department. It must have been several years since she had last checked the price tags for a gallon of interior satin, for her eyes bugged out as she swallowed hard. But those who know my wife know she isn't easily deterred. So, she approached the clerk and asked if she might have a word with the department manager. Now as random would have it, he was off this day. But the clerk said he'd get the sub, a manager on loan from another Home Depot yet.

Now was it Mari's Finnish accent that proved irresistible or random cosmic forces that surrounded her with good fortune? She opened the dialogue, *"A group of us started a church not so long ago and we just took ownership of a facility we want to freshen up. I'm noticing the cost of paint and being we're a new church, we're operating on a scanty budget."* (Point of fact, we weren't operating on any budget; can't budget what you don't have.) *"So, I'm wondering, may there be a chance that we could get a discount?"* I lean on the side that it was her accent that allured him.

Nevertheless, this surrogate manager introduced himself as *"Tim"* and explained why he was subbing this day - something that rarely occurred. He then asked, *"What's the name of your church?"*

Accommodatingly Mari replied, *"Faith Family Fellowship."*

He confessed he hadn't heard of us yet; but why would he? We had only recently celebrated out first birthday a few months back. He then asked, *"Do you have a pastor?"* Now was Tim being a cordial manager or was he that dissatisfied with his current job that he was probing a possible career change?

Mari simply answered, *"My husband."*

His ensuing question called for more than the obvious answer, *"Yes."* *"Does he have a name?"*

"Bob Hampton," Mari answered. Now if she had said, *"Tony Evans"* or *"James McDonald"* or *"Andy Stanley"*, then his response would've rang much truer. But when he said, *"Oh, I know Bob Hampton. I used to love to ..."* yada, yada, yada (that's Hebrew for *"what follows is pathetically insignificant."*)

What are the odds? A road construction that sent Mari to the Home Depot where she rarely shopped. The regular manager was out that day. And the pinch-hitting manager knew me. Nobody knows me! So, with this fusion of random occurrences, Tim then said he'd be *"back in a few minutes."* He explained he wanted to bounce something off his boss, which necessitated making a phone call. Tim wasn't gone five minutes when he returned with this unusual question, *"Will your husband be home tomorrow?"* Mari must've thought, *"Does that matter? How does my husband being at home get us paint from your store?"* Fortunately, Tim didn't protract Mari's confusion too long; he said, *"We'd like to see what all the project would entail and how Home Depot may be able to help. May I call your husband tomorrow?"* Because he proceeded to ask my wife for the number of walls and their dimensions, she interpreted his requests as a near-certainty of some amount of donation; perhaps even a hefty discount, one that would satisfy any shopper, particularly desperate ones like us.

Our phone rang at 10 the next morning. How long does it take to answer the phone when you're sitting right next to it? Keeping to his word, it was Tim. I had prepared some answers to a few questions I presumed he would ask; which he did. I provided him the square footage of our walls and I'd let the pro do the math to figure out how many gallons we would need. But then he asked an unanticipated question: *"Can my boss and I meet you at the church in a half hour?"*

("Say what? What was this all about? Maybe I misunderstood him? Meet at the church? Really? What for? Didn't he trust a minister's mathematical prowess to multiply height times width? Why must they see the place?") But no problem, *"Sure. I'll be there"*, assuming my heart, now clipping along at about 180bpm didn't explode under the excitement of this latest development. I arrived first because I had dropped everything I had been doing and wanted to personally greet them when they arrived. They weren't far behind. Immediately Tim pulled out a ledger with pen already in hand. I escorted his boss and him to the downstairs entrance – or so I thought. For as I turned around to begin sharing the story behind our gifted facility, they had already veered off at the first sidewalk intersection and proceeded to stroll around the property. I let them take their good ol' time. I wasn't about

to rush the donors of a gift horse and appear impatient. 10 minutes and several notes-on-the-ledger later, we entered the ground floor and I began giving them the inside tour – and the miracle story. They seemed as awed over our miracle as we had been, which afforded them even greater delight when they said, *"Can you be here tomorrow so our truck can drop off 40 bags of mulch* (they were 3 cu. ft. bags of red cedar), *and a large palate of paving stone so you can dress up the outside?"*

Now Mari's Finnish accent had certainly proved advantageous on previous occasions, but something much greater was operating behind the scenes once again. I said to my two benefactors, *"You've already gone way beyond graciousness in providing us the paint, but you're also throwing in mulch and pavers too??"* I thanked them profusely, while furtively shooting up a vertical word of thanks. Just when I had thought God had outdone Himself, He heaped another blessing atop our miracle blessing.

"About that paint –"

("Oh, I get it; here it comes. The mulch and the pavers are pacifying compensation for the paint you're not able to provide us. Someone back at Home Depot, and higher up, must've squelched the paint plan. But no big deal – really. They were still making better-than-good on quite a benevolent and totally-undeserved offer.")

"– you can pick that up as needed. Just go back to the paint department; we're keeping 40 gallons on the side for you."

"Forty gallons!" I erupted. Man, I was praying for six, maybe ten; but forty!!!

"You need to know something else," Tim stated eagerly. He had my undivided attention as I had no idea what he might come out with next. *"The most extraordinary thing happened immediately after your wife left my counter yesterday."* I was getting used to this phenomenon. No, not that I was becoming at all presumptuous! I was simply growing in

my view of God; how He so delights in displaying His All-sufficiency to those who humbly walk by faith. *"A man whom I had assumed was the next customer after your wife, stepped up to the counter and said to me, 'I couldn't help but overhear your conversation with that woman. I'm the Glidden rep for this store and I'm in from Ohio for my semi-annual inventory check. Glidden would like to pick up the tab for all the paint she needs."* If you bend toward a more skeptic view of the supernatural, you must be scratching your head about now. Certainly, you pieced together that the odds of this path intersection can't be even a blip on the random cosmic radar screen. The Glidden representative who visits this store but twice per year, just happened to approach the paint section at the exact time of day that this almost-never visitor offered her impassioned plea for discount consideration to a rarely-in-the-store substitute manager who happened to know me. Now either my God is Sovereign over all the events surrounding our lives and orchestrates them to effect His Overall Purposes, or our church needs to start playing the lottery.

The Home Depot truck pulled onto our lot the following day and unloaded the promised paraphernalia. Over the ensuing month, I paid more than a couple of visits to the paint department. With several volunteer hands, a fresh coat of paint on virtually everything interior soon graced our place. *"Simple, but beautiful"* resounded throughout.

Everyone who espouses a sincere and abiding trust in God applauds His perspicacious Handwriting on our building's halls and walls. How can we not? For He has clearly scripted for all who enter, *"I did this."* And for any who may question, *"Why?"* the answer is as evident as the painted walls and mulched gardens: because God delights in pouring out His Undeserved Favor on those who by His Spirit strive to *"walk by faith, not by sight."*

A gifted building and gifted accoutrements, the climactic couplet that could well serve as the natural place to conclude the story of Faith

Family Fellowship. But I fear I may be sending any readers a message that fails to provide a proper perspective on "seeing" God through this parade of miracles. Yes, our church has witnessed some incredible displays of His Awesome Sovereignty (what diehard skeptics would cling to as random cosmic occurrences. But what alternative explanations could they possibly offer that wouldn't require even greater measures of faith in something other than a God of Infinite Love?) But God has chosen to do these supernatural works amid FFF as part of His Overarching Plan. Our church is no more special than any other church that seeks to extol the God of the Bible. As surely as we have experienced the indescribable, I can assert that every church has received its parade of Divine interventions too. However, because we live in the day of Disney World, multimillion dollar pyrotechnic displays and America's Got Talent, we expect to be wowed at every venue and experience. Only the truly incredible moves us anymore. Churches too have been caught up in this spectacular-expectation mentality, even giving justification for such under the salving umbrella of cultural relevance. We feel we must put on a show for the audience, and if we fail, then our "worship" service isn't successful. May I remind the Christian community Who is the True Audience at such gatherings. Do we really think any church can wow Him Who is the Author of WOW? Reality dictates that anything truly spectacular emanates from His end and not ours - and not just at worship services. In ages past, He parted the Red Sea to begin a nation. In recent days, He spoke through a dying man to conceive a church and dropped a deed in an offering plate to give it life.

The greater message I want to send, however, extends way beyond those undeniable Divine manifestations of His Glory. God has also dotted Faith Family Fellowship's chronology with "lesser" miracles along our four-year journey; the kind so common to all churches that believe God still performs miracles. But I fear the routine of His Daily

Interventions have become so familiar, that our familiarity has bred, not contempt, but complacency. I'm often encouraged by something God reminds His own: *"We have not, because we ask not."* But I'm also encouraged by something I must routinely remind myself, *"We have, but we see not."* Every day God is peppering our church landscapes with Divine Visits; but are we "seeing" these "unremarkable" miracles? Because our human proclivity yearns for the remarkable variety, we may be missing the daily parade of the unspectacular kind. Now understand, both are equally glorious – and for the same reason. Both issue from the One Who is Himself Glorious and so orchestrates life's *"Random Cosmic Occurrences"* into the convincing proof that He is God and He alone! Six of my favorite "lesser" FFF Eddie-Face miracles will serve as testament to the Glory of God's unremarkable visitations.

Our first "lesser" miracle won't seem "lesser" at all to people of faith - because of the timing involved in this one. On July 18th, Faith Family Fellowship received the deed that sealed the deal on our miracle building. Was it on that same day or just within a few days that Big Ed and his wife, Karen, received a totally unexpected piece of mail? An insurance company had been trying to track Ed down to grant him the payout from a modest life insurance policy his son had taken out. Ed had no clue it even existed. Parents pray their children bury them as opposed to the alternative. In this case, Ed buried his son after being tragically killed in an auto accident - 19 years prior! The company must have been government operated. Was this another Random Cosmic Occurrence that this payout came 19 years after the fact, but within days of the need? Ed and Karen gifted 25% of their surprise to the church to be earmarked for several items on a "Needs List" created by the Leadership Team, including a First Aid Kit and two children's tables with chairs. No insurance payout ever erases the grief for having lost a loved one; but perhaps in Ed's grief, a sense of good arising out of tragedy will help ease the hurt.

Our second "lesser" miracle may be lesser in terms of its miraculous nature, but it's anything but lesser in terms of its essential import to our very existence. Whenever someone receives a gift horse, we all know it's not something you look in the mouth. How much more so when that someone equals an entire church of someone's! We received our quaint, old building from the magnanimous generosity of a retired couple. But the property as it existed, provided very little parking. I soon mapped out a to-scale representation to see how we could accommodate this obvious need. Now I'm no architect, much less an artist; but after some proposed landscape alterations, I managed to squeeze 21 parking spaces onto our postage-stamp lot - and one hitching post for six horses for those who wished to recapture the nostalgia of the church's early years. I marched proudly into our local municipal office to request permission from the Planning Board. I wasn't prepared for their response as they instructed me to contact our state Department of Transportation. (*"Why would I need to do this? What jurisdiction could it possibly have over our property?"*) As it turned out, more than I wanted to learn.

Our new gift perches on the northeast corner of a country intersection. The front of our building faces a county road while our parking-lot side of the building faces a state road. *"So, we get more visibility, right?"* Probably - but we get no parking, nada, zilch, not even a single handicapped spot. (I even formerly requested an exception to this prohibition - to no avail.)

So now what do we do? We have this gift building that is being restored to its original purpose for being a gathering place for corporate worship. But we must tell all our people that they must walk to worship - except for the six who can ride their horse and park it at the hitching post. As for marketing our church to the greater community in the hope that many would visit, I was struggling how to make our pitch inviting: *"We're your new neighbor. Please come and exercise your heart in worship with us. And while you're at it, exercise your whole body by walking ..."* I experimented with, *"We're your new neighbor. Please come and worship with us. We provide valet service from your doorstep to ours."* If I wasn't buying any of this, how could our church family? How could the greater community? The bottom line came down to this: we owned a building, but we were denied an Occupancy Permit without off-site parking.

Now I don't know how many houses dotted the landscape surrounding our church when it was first erected in 1873. What I do know is it was a residential community. A century and a half later, little has changed, except the number of houses. A casual stroll through the neighborhood in all four directions validates this. Just within walking distance are 50 homes. So how will these 50 houses address our parking need? 50 driveways? This wouldn't be a miracle; this would be a mess.

("Well how about any businesses in the neighborhood?") Maybe they have a *lot* to offer? There are but two within a mile radius that could provide sufficient parking. Herein is the miracle: both sit catty-corner across the street from our church. So, my next task necessitated I convince their owners how great a service they would be to our shared community - and at an affordable price for a fledgling church, whose offering plate held a deed, but limited dollars. I arranged to meet separately with Randy Beck, of Beck's Land & Sea House and Jan Jennings-Ochs of Jennings Transportation, Inc. Both proved to be (and continue to be) welcoming and friendly people; but these attributes don't necessarily signal they will be reasonable. Well they weren't. Reasonable would mean they would charge us a lease fee that our few families could afford. Instead, they chose to charge us nothing!

(Initially, one charged a very affordable fee, but for a brief time till our church proved responsible in using its lot.)

Skeptics may fail to see the "miracle" in this provision, but those of us who park our cars week after week in one of these lots to make the 50-100 steps to our property, appreciate it as nothing less. One little church in a near-total residential area, sitting across the street from the only two businesses in sight; sounds like a strategically Divine placement to me. There are bigger churches with their own parking lots where the congregants must walk further.

A gift-horse building, but with no parking - until Beck's and Jennings! And like the building itself, totally free! What an additional blessing from our two very gracious neighbors.

The third of our "lesser" miracles, takes us to the doorstep of our inaugural worship service we had scheduled for October 5th. We were near set to soar, having painted most of the interior. It looked simply beautiful - except that is, for the dais. That looked simply beastly. The front third held promise, appearing salvageable, assuming there weren't too many layers of stain. Perhaps with some serious elbow grease, the original pine would show off its original charm. The back two-thirds, however, held no promise whatsoever. Warped and moldy, this portion of patchwork plywood beckoned to be tossed atop the trash heap.

Meantime, one of our founding families broke us the good-for-them, bad-for-us news that they were relocating to the Sunshine state at the beginning of November. Best time to *dodge* out of Pennsylvania. So, while the church family was decorating its new home, Dave and Beth were emptying out their old one. For the entire month of October, they packed and visited local family and friends before their move. Consequently, they never got to see but at a glance, the refurbishing that had gone on in our building.

Relocations always signal a winnowing process - what gets packed and what gets sacked. Dave called me one afternoon and asked if the church could use a carpet. An indoor-outdoor tweed that was like new, but with wall-to-wall in their new home, it became obsolete. Immediately my mind pictured the perfect spot for it, especially with the heavy traffic of our praise band. However, what were its dimensions? What was the color? I asked if I could check it out before I made any decision. No problem.

I can abbreviate here by saying the color was perfectly neutral, a two-tone light brown that accentuated our beige walls. As for the size, it perfectly matched the width of our stage. Not only did it cover the entire, eyesore plywood, but it nestled right up to the edge of the two-inch finished trim on both sides. The depth overlapped the newly-polyurethaned pine wood a mere four inches. We could live with that.

The fourth "lesser" miracle addressed our need for a specific piece of furniture. Every church needs a nursery if it hopes to grow. Young families seeking a "home church" won't give a second look at a church that doesn't provide satisfactory children's facilities and programs. We didn't wish to be listed among the "Once-and-Done" visitation list. All infants and most toddlers need rocking now and again – especially when pastors go long on the wind. I felt a rocking chair was the logical solution, so I spread the word. Certainly, somebody in our church family had a rocking chair that wasn't rocking these days, sitting idle in some former nursery or sewing room. I didn't pray to God to fill this need because somebody in our church family could and would. Two weeks later, I began to pray.

Yard sales are big in our area, entire lawns stuffed with the host family's trash, but another family's soon-to-be-treasures. Typically, these are held on weekends. This was a weekday, so there would be no Yard Sales this day. But it didn't really matter as Mari wasn't in a flea-marketing mood. She was headed to "Promised Land" where she volunteered her time escorting special needs children alongside therapeutic horses. Besides, Mari and I both have been to our fair share of Yard Sales over the years, and neither of us ever remember seeing a single rocker ticketed to go. But in that short commute from our house to the riding rink, she happened to glance down a side street as she was passing it. *("Did I just see what I thought I saw?")* Her hairpin 180, defying every law of physics, certainly argued she had. There was no way she wasn't going to check this out. *("Had this family's grandma been sitting curbside on this rocker peeling potatoes and took her produce back to the house? Or was one of their kids selling lemonade, but needed to take a break? Or was this aged rocking chair destined for the furniture pyre with a broken leg?)* Mari pulled along the curb. Not only was it what she thought she had seen, a rocking chair, but it cradled a sign that read, *"Free!"* (Our church was being spoiled by *"free."*)

Mari's car couldn't squeeze FFF's newest "baby" in the back of her car so she promptly phoned me and gave me directions that required no *"Recalculating."* As I flew out the door, I grabbed a bottle of *"Old English."* Within a few minutes, we were together positioning our adoption in my hatchback. From there I went straight to the church and after a liberal application of scratch guard, our newest addition looked near-new. We named him, *"Rock and Soul."*

The fifth unremarkable miracle took place on an ordinary Sunday morning. Before the worship hour began, I observed a set of new faces, already nestled in a back-row pew. Walking over to them, I extended my hand, greeted them and introduced myself in typical fashion. *"Hi, I'm Bob."* In small churches where everyone knows everyone else, visitors can't evade notice. So, with a few minutes before the Praise Band invited us to join them inside Heaven's Throne Room, I asked a question to which I already knew the answer. The man responded with, *"Yes, this is our first visit."* I followed with the question that can no longer be assumed. He said, *"Yes, I'm Steve and this is my wife, Marie."* We exchanged some further superficial pleasantries, but none more ear-catching to a small church than that they were more than just visiting, they were hunting. Several months back they had decided to leave their home church of 20 years and find a new one. I concluded our introduction with something in the order of, *"I trust you enjoy your worship experience with us today."* Then after the service, I invited them to our Fellowship Hour in our downstairs Family Hall. They graciously declined, but did say that they'd be back next week. Evidently what they saw and felt that day earned us a second look.

Sure enough, not only did Steve and Marie return, they sat in the same section of the same pew. I greeted them by name because people that leave a good impression are remembered. They had left a very good impression as a couple who displayed a sincere desire to please Jesus. By the end of that service, they had concluded their search for a new church home was over – and told me so. I shared my delight, first with them and then with the One they so desired to please.

I can't remember if it was before or after the service the following Sunday that Steve asked me a ne'er-before asked question by a newcomer. After 35 years in ministry, I had heard such usual questions as, *"Do you have small groups?"*, *"What form of church government do you practice?"* and *"Do you dribble or dunk?"* a question that cared nothing for my Michael Jordan b-ball prowess, but for our church's baptismal mode. In sharp contrast to all the usual early questions, Steve asked, *"Did I hear you're putting up a church sign?"*

Earlier I disclosed my hearing deficit. Obviously, it was rearing its ugly ear once again. So, I answered his question with an astute one of my own, *"I'm sorry; what did you say?"*

"Did I hear you're putting up a church sign outside?"

Oh, now I got it. *"A church sign, yes."* My cognitive wheels were doing Figure-8's trying to figure out what in God's Great Kingdom was this all about. Steve didn't abandon me for long in my own ecclesiastical musings.

"When will it be completed?"

"My neighbor two doors up creates signs for a living. He finished it just last week."

"Who's installing it?"

("Wait a minute. Boko Haram is kidnapping who knows how many young women to who knows where to do who knows what. ISIS is promising to unite its most faithful soldiers with a heavenly harem. North Korea is testing nuclear warheads with threats they could reach our west coast. And Asia Bibi still languishes in some Pakistani hell-hole prison. And you want to know who's digging the holes for our new church sign?) I was back to not getting it. Nevertheless, I answered with usual Bob Hampton humor – which many would classify otherwise. *"Well, I've assigned my wife to the task. But if the ground is as riddled with shale beneath the surface as it is on the surface - I may help her."* I laughed at my own joke. I alone. I tend to be the only one who ever does. *"Actually, I've got a team of guys meeting here on Saturday morning to put it in."*

"What time?" Steve pressed.

"Shortly after 8; depending on how long it takes us to mount it on George's trailer." I told him George and his wife, Karen, were two of our most recent church additions.

Steve's retort showcased the second unremarkable Divine miracle. *"I'll bring over two of my men and have the hole dug by the time you arrive."* Steve quickly dispelled all my confusion-fog. *"I own a fence company and I'll bring over my hydraulic posthole diggers."*

Process the timing. If this fence-man had first visited the following Sunday, Mari would've been exhausted and sore from all her digging – and I'd be in the doghouse - again. Well, probably neither; but the sign would have already been mounted. Or if Steve had first visited just the week prior, he wouldn't have overheard the conversation that disclosed our sign plan. Or if Steve had visited any weeks prior to his initial visit, he would've likely been an integral part of the sign discussion. So, nothing particularly remarkable about that. But Steve had first visited two weeks prior, just in the improbably Sovereign nick of time to be Divinely positioned to volunteer his expertise for the benefit of FFF's practical need. What an amazing God Who sent another ripple down His steady stream of verifications, proving He always works in our de – fence!

One final "lesser" miracle continues to sculpt a smile on my face - every single Sunday morning. Now I suspect most, even among people of faith, won't perceive this as a miracle. But it is to me. And why? Because I think the best miracles surface not with deeds dropped in offering plates or 40 gallons of paint being delivered to doorsteps or even with Divine words spilling out from a dying man's lips. I believe the best miracles are witnessed in changed lives.

This miracle that still moves me takes us back to the days immediately following the close on our new building. I was working on the landscape to dress it up in the hopes it would attract neighborhood attention. It did - on the very first day I was out there. 70-something year old Karin, who lived right next door, came walking up, introduced herself and inquired about what was going on with the property. She knew the former residents, but was thrilled to learn it was about to become a church again. Was it her love of history that couldn't see a church building used for any other purpose than as a church? She made it clear that our church was doing the right thing. I chuckled within.

I stopped chuckling within when Karin started telling me all I needed to do to get the place looking right - being translated meant, how she pictured it. The list proved rather lengthy - and I was already in my late 50's. I wasn't sure I would live long enough to get it all done.

It's what Karin said next that stopped me in my tracks - and near stopped my heart in its rhythm. She didn't simply request a tour of the facility; she had seen the inside a handful of times when the Face's resided there. She let me know, however, she had never been inside the steeple - but she wanted to be. I'll be the first to say, having already been in it myself, it provides a panoramic sweep of the beautiful countryside of Upper Nazareth. I attempted several deflections to hopefully discourage her interest. No matter what rationale or tactic I used, she remained undeterred. Finally, I conceded as I didn't wish to make an enemy of our closest neighbor. I did insist on one thing though: she let me climb behind her. You need to understand that this steeple can only be accessed by climbing a ladder, a steep ladder, and one without a lot of shoulder space to navigate. I explained this to Karin. I figured if she lost her footing, I could at least break her fall - as I broke my neck. Her response: *"So, are you inferring I'm not physically fit - or I'm too old. I'm from good ol' German stock. I survived the war"* (I knew which one she meant) *"so climbing a ladder won't be a problem."*

It wasn't. She scaled that ladder faster and more fluidly than some twenty-something year olds climb into bed at night. Do you remember those final words Humphrey Bogart spoke to Captain Renault at the close of the 1942 Best Picture, *Casablanca?* How aptly they fit for Karin and me: *"Louie, I think this is the beginning of a beautiful friendship."* It really was - and has been. But what stands preeminent in my mind about our friendship has been her servant's heart I've witnessed from the first Sunday we opened our doors. This one-time impromptu foreman has reflected what we treasure most in the lives of all our church family members - to be servants in the likeness of Jesus Himself. Karin is certainly this - and so is Gail and Deb and Ed and everybody else. Now you know why I treasure this miracle as the best one of all. I get to rub shoulders every day with Jesus lookalikes.

Epilogue

Just this past Saturday (from the vantage point of my final revision), Faith Family Fellowship celebrated its fourth birthday by conducting our monthly worship service at the very place we held our first. As always, the service blessed the seasoned residents of Alexandria Manor; and perhaps more so than usual because Mari brought the message that morning. But for those of us from the church, the service proved to be especially gratifying. We were reflecting with deep awe and appreciation for how richly God has showered us with His Presence and Provision throughout our brief history. We have not taken His Generosity and Grace lightly or for granted. We know He owes us nothing. Just in giving us life in His Son is more than we could ever ask for, much less deserve. Nevertheless, for whatever His purposes, He has love-tapped us with two miracles more extraordinary than most Christians will ever see in their lifetimes: His Prophetic Voice thundering through Ray's last words and His Magnanimous Gift of the deed through the Face's selfless offering. But He hasn't stopped there. He keeps on love-tapping us with "lesser" miracles that mean as much to us as His grand kisses.

We believe God is love-tapping us even as I bring our miracle-story to a close. Our gifted-building's false brick exterior has been deteriorating over who knows how many years. Soon rainwater will forge a series of pathways into the interior - and this is a baptism we don't want. So, we are giving our building a facelift to preserve it long beyond my days; all the while sustaining our *"simple, but beautiful"* motif. So, where's the love-tap in this? God will provide the finances to complete the project. We don't yet know how - or when; we just know. We are convinced that He didn't bring us into our Promised Land to then send us off into exile in the wilderness. He's going to see this project through and many more besides. We believe this, because as with me, so too with our church: He's not finished with us yet!

Yes, the "us" includes me. God's not done with me yet either; He has more for me to do. I don't know how much more or for how long. But in looking back over the past 17 years, I stand amazed that He took this eminent failure and privileged me to succeed! No, my spiritual journey isn't over, and I could fail again, but I've grown in my grasp of God. He's no quitter. He never says about His own, *"I'm so done with this guy. He's such a loser."* God grants 2nd chances, 3rd chances, multiple chances to those who keep tripping up, but who eventually look up to plead and accept His Boundless Mercy and Grace.

I may never again witness even one remarkable miracle like the two I've seen at FFF. But like that late Saturday afternoon in 2013 as I stood aside my wife in our kitchen, I still don't ask for a sign. But unlike that day, I don't even ask for *"a little direction right about now"*. Why? Because in my multiple chances, God is helping me put into daily practice something I've always preached: *"We walk by faith, not by sight."* And as I have, I'm seeing a whole lot better. In this regard, I'm seeing an extraordinarily moist triple chocolate sheet cake with lavishly thick milk chocolate icing - *"simple, but beautifully"* adorned with five, joyous church birthday candles.

CPSIA information can be obtained
at www.ICGtesting.com
Printed in the USA
BVOW06s0241231217
503486BV00006B/8/P